UnCURABLE

From Hopeless Diagnosis
to Defying All Odds

Aaron Hartman, MD

LEGACY
launch pad
PUBLISHING

ISBN: [978-1-968339-13-5] (ebook)

ISBN: [978-1-968339-14-2] (paperback)

ISBN: [978-1-968339-15-9] (hardcover)

DISCLAIMERS

Important medical disclaimer: Look, I'm a licensed physician, but I'm not *YOUR* physician—there's a big difference. This book aims to educate and inform you, not to replace the relationship you have with your own healthcare provider. I can't diagnose you through these pages, and I definitely can't treat you from here. Every person's medical situation is unique, so before you make any changes to your treatment, diet or lifestyle based on what you read here, please talk to your own qualified healthcare provider first. That's just smart medicine.

Privacy disclaimer: The stories you'll read in this book are real—they come from my years of clinical experience. But I've changed names, identifying details and sometimes combined different patients' experiences to protect everyone's privacy. Some of the people you'll "meet" are actually composites. The conversations and events have been recreated to give you the essence of what happened, not a word-for-word transcript. Real life is messy, and I've cleaned it up a bit to help you learn.

∽

For more information about Dr. Aaron Hartman and *UnCurable*, scan the QR code below

DEDICATION

For my daughter Anna,
my wife Becky
and the patients who taught me to listen...

*Anna at four years old doing suit therapy
(i.e., dynamic compression suit with elastic resistance).*

TABLE OF CONTENTS

PREFACE

I can still remember the first time I saw Anna—it's etched into my mind like it happened just yesterday. We had just stepped into her foster home where she was receiving care. There she was, on the floor of the living room, sitting in a Bumbo chair placed gently on a Winnie the Pooh blanket, her tiny body leaned forward, unable to support itself. A patch covered her "strong" right eye—not because it was injured, but because the left eye had suffered birth trauma so severe it no longer functioned, so it was a struggle for her eyes to track together. Her delicate hands were curled inward, held tightly to her chest—all symptoms of the lingering, visible imprint of the brain damage she'd endured over a year ago during birth.

Despite everything, she had the cutest little smile. The only word she could say was "hi."

She was about 12 months old at that time, and I had no idea how profoundly this moment would change my life. Meeting Anna would not only change me, but it would also shape my family, influence how my family grew and ultimately transform my medical practice and how I cared for patients.

Anna had been diagnosed with cerebral palsy, an incurable condition caused by brain damage before birth. But that wasn't all.

Her birth mother had used crystal meth throughout her entire pregnancy, and Anna had suffered a stroke before she was even born. She had no pigment in the back of her eyes and was functionally blind for the first years of her life. She spent those early months in a drug-induced coma, not interacting with the outside world other than when being fed. An earlier MRI showed that she had agenesis of the corpus callosum—meaning the part of the brain that connects the left and right hemispheres hadn't formed properly. When I first met her, I didn't fully grasp the severity of her condition. All I knew was that she had an incurable disorder and was about to lose her home.

My wife, Becky, had been Anna's occupational therapist ever since she left the hospital. Like many medical foster children, Anna was facing yet another upheaval—her foster home was closing, and she needed a new place to live. Becky asked me if we would be willing to open our home to this little girl who had nowhere else to go.

As a person of faith, this was a defining moment. I had always professed to believe in caring for the orphaned and the homeless, and now I was being given the opportunity to live out those beliefs. Meanwhile, Becky saw something that no one else did: a spark in Anna—something neither the doctors nor the therapists, nor even I, could see. Becky told me, "She's going to be okay." Looking back, I realize that I thought "okay" meant that her condition would somehow disappear and that she would become a normal, typical child. In hindsight, that was incredibly naïve. But I trusted Becky, and I had my faith. So we took Anna into our home.

As a doctor, I knew it'd be rough. My brain cataloged the challenges ahead—sleepless nights, medical complexities and mounting bills. I have to admit that in the beginning, my heart wasn't immediately wrapped around this little girl. My connection to Anna was forged through battle—the daily struggle of coaxing one more bite into her mouth, celebrating small movements in therapy and standing firm against specialists who only saw her limitations. My heart expanded as I defended her, fought for her future and refused to accept the low expectations she had been saddled with. I truly fell in love with Anna over that first year of advocacy. My faith may have led me to her, but the daily fight to believe in and help her reach her full potential transformed her from a responsibility to my daughter— my little girl.

Bringing Anna home with us was our "inch at Cape Canaveral" that became our "mile at the moon" moment. What I mean is that this one small decision changed everything. Yes, Anna has changed me spiritually and emotionally, but the moment we opened our lives to her also reshaped me professionally. That decision changed how I viewed the healthcare system, how I saw the interactions between specialists and parents, how I understood trauma in children and even how I conducted research and applied it to my patients. It changed my entire approach to medicine. Now, more than 18 years later, I can look back and see that this small step transformed every-thing—not just for me and my medical practice, but for Anna.

Healthcare has a history of blind spots. We got smoking wrong for over half a century—it took 7000 research articles before the Surgeon General of the United States finally stated that smoking caused lung cancer. We got it wrong in the first half of the 20th century when we performed frontal lobotomies to treat mental health conditions and radical mastectomies to treat minimally inva-sive breast cancer. More recently, since the year 2000 we have incor-rectly understood and practiced hormonal therapy for women, and it is only in the last year of this writing (2025) that this life-changing therapy is once again "allowed" for use with menopausal women. The question I constantly ask myself is, "Where are our system's current blind spots?" What are we wrong about now that in 20 years we will view as the "antiquated past"? About what will we say, in a superior voice, "Can you believe those doctors used to...?" I wonder.

But I do have some ideas about it.

Anna's needs and treatment were a blind spot to the health professionals that cared for her. Today she has defied every single expectation. She was a child who was born blind and was never supposed to see. She was never supposed to crawl, walk or talk. The healthcare system had set the bar so low for her that even the therapists who worked with her (and cared deeply for her) saw little hope for this child with brain damage and cerebral palsy.

But Anna's story is one of overcoming every obstacle placed in her path. It is a story of breaking the mold, defying the experts and refusing to accept limitations. It is a story of a family that surrounded her with love and fought for her. It is a story of a father who woke up at 4 am to research cerebral palsy, autism, gene-based nutrition, drug-induced brain damage, hyperbaric oxygen therapy, energy therapy and a host of other treatments that would become part of Anna's healing journey.

Built on the foundations of functional medicine, real food, a loving family, quality sleep and exercise, these interventions have produced nothing short of a miracle. At 19 years old, Anna can read. She can text on the phone. She spends hours a day talking and singing to her grandparents on the phone. She manages most of her own self-care. She is a joy to be around and has an infectious laugh. What's even more remarkable is that every year, she continues to improve. This is unheard of in the special needs world for a child with her diagnoses.

And the message I have for you is this: If Anna can do it, you can do it too!

Anna's story is one of hope. It is a testament to what is possible when you step outside the constraints of conventional medicine, forge your own path and build a personalized healthcare approach. It is about healing in situations deemed hopeless. If Anna can do it, you can too. That is the message of this book.

So come alongside us. Let me introduce you to my family. Let me introduce you to Anna. Learn what we did. And as you turn these pages, I want you to realize that if this little girl could beat the odds, nothing is stopping you from doing the same—whatever that means for you. For the Hartman family, beating the odds and going against the grain has become a way of life. We take one step at a time, one day at a time, one intervention at a time. You have the same potential, and over time you will also see unimaginable results and a transformation in your health.

INTRODUCTION
FROM CONVENTIONAL MEDICINE TO COMPREHENSIVE WELLNESS

I never expected my medical career to take such a wild turn. I started out as a regular family doctor: I graduated with top honors in biology from Virginia Commonwealth University in 1995, then I received my MD from the Medical College of Virginia in 2000. I was on the usual path most doctors tread, finishing my residency and getting board-certified.

Then I had to fulfill my military commitments. My time in the Air Force from 2003 to 2007 really shaped me. I became a Major, ran a clinic in Germany and became medical supervisor of a clinic at MacDill Air Force Base, Tampa, Florida. I even got extra training in dermatology, cardiology and nuclear/biological warfare during this time. I was on track to have a typical, successful medical career.

But life had other plans for me. When my wife Becky and I brought Anna into our home, I initially responded to her medical needs by following the conventional methods—dutifully going through the motions of appointments, filling prescriptions and following specialists' recommendations. Yet beneath the surface, I felt increasingly helpless and discouraged by our limited options. As I searched for ways to truly help our little girl, I encountered rigid barriers within conventional medicine—a systemic resistance to outside-the-box thinking and a concerning lack of curiosity about alternative approaches. When experts dismissed what I had discovered as promising treatment options without investigation, I realized I was facing more than just our daughter's medical challenges; I was confronting the limitations of the medical system itself. It became clear that to help her, I needed to think differently, venturing beyond traditional boundaries into unexplored territory.

This personal crisis became professional and sparked my deep dive into integrative and functional medicine. I started using new ideas to treat not just my daughter but other family members as well and eventually my patients in my medical practice. I became more active in medical education. In 2011, I became an assistant Clinical Professor in Family Medicine at the Virginia Commonwealth University's School of Medicine. In 2010, I started the Virginia Research Center, a clinical research company where we offered new treatment options through FDA-approved clinical trials. And I just kept learning.

In 2012, I made it official by joining several national medical organizations and starting a training program in functional medicine. That same year, our journey with Anna led us to some unexpected places. Becky and I moved our family to a small farm near Richmond, Virginia where we have learned how our health connects to the land, animals and food. This got me really excited about nutrition, ecology and toxicology in medicine.

In 2015 and 2016, I earned certifications in integrative and functional medicine, which meant I could help my patients in ways I never thought possible, and I capped off this season in my life with my third board certification in metabolic, regenerative, anti-aging and functional medicine in 2022.

Today, I lead Richmond Integrative & Functional Medicine, a practice I founded in 2016 with a clear mission: to transform each patient's health in a truly individualized way using my extensive research, medical expertise and personal experience. Inspired by the astonishing response of my daughter, I am committed to helping others achieve similar life-changing results. This powerful approach

—often called functional medicine, translational medicine or root cause medicine—goes beyond treating symptoms to uncover and address the true underlying causes of illness, empowering people to reclaim their health and vitality.

My story encompasses both work and family. Becky and I adopted three kids between 2007 and 2016. Being foster parents and then adoptive parents has made our lives so much richer, but it's been ridiculously hard. If my work and our story can make any part of your health journey any easier, then all the work will have been worth it.

Over the past 25 years, I've been privileged to care for patients in more than 100000 clinical encounters spanning four continents. My work has extended far beyond everyday practice—I've contributed to over 70 clinical trials and published research in *The Lancet*, one of medicine's most prestigious journals. In my seminary thesis, I deeply explored how faith, work and compassion can intersect to enrich learning and knowledge. Yet through all these professional accomplishments, my core drive has remained unchanged: first, to help Anna overcome her challenges; then, to apply those insights to improve my family's health; and finally, to use this hard-won knowledge to achieve better outcomes for my patients. Everything I've learned has flowed from that initial commitment to one little girl who defied the odds.

This book serves as a guide to true wellness, based on my personal and professional experiences. It's about the path we forged to health that goes beyond just treating symptoms. I will show you our path, so that you can follow our lead, eventually forging your own path to reach your own health potential—and you will probably surprise yourself along the way, just as Anna consistently amazes us. Together, we'll explore how you can take control of your health, just like I helped my daughter, my wife and countless patients get better. You'll learn how to unblock your health obstacles and get your energy back. This book will show you how to defy the odds and create your own health success story.

UnCurable is Anna's story of resilience, courage and fortitude. It is a guide for anyone facing a tough medical diagnosis. It's for those who feel let down by our healthcare system and want a holistic approach to healing.

In this book, you'll discover:

- How a wake-up call can lead to transformative change in healthcare practices
- Why battling a broken system might be necessary for you or your loved one's health
- The power of faith in action when combined with cutting-edge medical approaches
- What this looks like in other real patient success stories
- How you can take ownership of your health and shape the future of medicine
- Ways to rethink conventional wisdom about "uncurable" conditions
- The unexpected impact of lifestyle changes on complex medical cases
- Why challenging medical dogma might be the key to breakthrough healing
- How to navigate bureaucratic roadblocks in the healthcare system
- The surprising connection between faith, science and medical innovation

This book invites you to join us on a journey of hope, strength and healing. It's a call to action for patients, doctors and anyone who thinks there's more to health than what normal medicine offers. Let's challenge the idea of "uncurable" together.

Throughout this book, I reference the same tools and resources I use every day in my clinic—the very ones that have helped transform the lives of my patients and my own family. These aren't generic tips or theoretical ideas. They are field-tested, fine-tuned frameworks I've spent years building, refining and sharing with people just like you— people facing overwhelming diagnoses and looking for real hope and real answers. I've also provided the sources for my research—studies, journals, books and publications—as this is an important part of medical research. You will read about how the medical system is far from perfect, but there is so much value in understanding and respecting the research performed and published by experts in their fields.

At the end of each chapter, you'll find a QR code that links to a custom landing page filled with curated resources related to what you just read. These might include patient handouts, deep-dive articles, tools for advocacy, videos or worksheets—practical tools designed to help you put this knowledge into action right away.

These resources are free to you—and I invite you to use them, revisit them and share them. My hope is that they'll be as life-changing for you as they've been for my daughter, my patients and my own health journey.

If you want a more complete and thorough bio about me, my training and credentials, you can find that on my website, here: **AaronHartmanMD.com**

∿

PART I

THE WAKE UP CALL

1

THE STATUS QUO, INTERRUPTED

The moment we adopted Anna, everything I thought I knew about medicine was put to the test.

–Dr. Aaron Hartman

Beep, beep, beep.

The rhythmic sound of monitors fills the NICU, blending with the sharp scent of disinfectant. Behind the glass of an incubator lies a tiny, fragile baby—Anna. Born too soon, too small, fighting battles before she even knew the world. But I didn't meet her then. That moment wouldn't come until a year later —when everything I thought I knew about medicine would be put to the test.

When I met Anna, my world flipped upside down. My medical degree no longer meant anything. Those years of training failed to prepare me for this tough, resilient, broken little girl. You too are about to go on a wild ride that will likely shake up everything you think you know about medicine. You'll find out why top doctors were so wrong about Anna, and you'll realize they might be missing something about you or your loved ones as well.

This part of the book serves as both a story and a wake-up call in print. You'll see the medical world in a whole new way. You'll start to question dogma and challenge the way things are done. This is all good! In order to go down an alternate path to healing, the old paradigms have to be shaken up a bit, or maybe even completely remade.

So let's walk through medical school together. That's where they teach us to trust the system, to obey authority and value prestige. You'll also sit with me as I watch that system fail Anna over and over. You'll get fired up when you realize that sometimes, being a good doctor means breaking the rules.

Many people accept the status quo as the final word; *That's just how it is,* we say to ourselves, unknowingly complicit in maintaining a broken system. Forget that. You're about to learn why we sometimes need to go around the medical rules, rewrite them or throw them out.

You'll learn about the things medicine has missed for years. You'll cringe at old medical mistakes—like cutting into brains to fix mental health or removing entire reproductive systems for cancer.

But this book isn't just about pointing out problems. It's about finding new ways to help people. Personalized healthcare is a crucial concept with real importance. You'll learn about new treatments that could change lives. Treatments that some doctors might call "impossible" or "unproven." Just like they said Anna couldn't get better.

This book is going to tell you to question everything. To take charge of your health like never before. Because if Anna taught me one thing, it's that our bodies and spirits can do amazing things. We just need the right tools and direction.

You'll find out why doctors, even when they try their best, don't know everything. You'll see why the system sometimes works against the people it's supposed to help. And most importantly, you'll learn why your health and your life is too important to leave only in other people's hands.

By the end, you'll see doctors' offices differently. You'll go in ready with questions and not afraid to speak up for yourself and your family. That's what I had to do for Anna. And that's what changed everything.

Listen, you're about to have your mind blown. You're going to see medicine in a whole new light—not as a set of rigid protocols, but as a dynamic journey of discovery. What doctors label "impossible" might just be the starting point of what's achievable. The same system that told Anna she'd never walk, talk or thrive has been proven wrong time and again—not just with her, but with countless patients who refused to accept someone else's prescribed limitations as their doomed destiny. But this isn't about rejecting science; it's about taking what is known, expanding it and pushing boundaries until a breakthrough happens.

A quick word about the title of this book: I am trying to turn the idea of "uncurable" on its head. When we adopted Anna, we were told her health conditions were absolute, and that there was no cure for any of her health complications we would inevitably encounter. As you'll read, we rejected the idea that she was "uncurable," and eventually I learned with my patients that "uncurable" is not a diagnosis. I want my family, my patients and you to abandon this word and its limitations, and to empower yourself by focusing instead on "curable."

Whether you're a practitioner, an advocate or a patient, by the time you finish this book, you'll no longer see "uncurable" as a sentence, but as a challenge—one that you're fully equipped to confront. Get ready to rewrite medical expectations, reclaim your power and prove everyone wrong—including the voice in your head that whispers, "Maybe this is as good as it gets." It's not.

The revolution starts now. Let's shake things up. Let's rewrite what's possible. Welcome to the rebellion.

Scan the QR code below with your phone's camera. This will direct you to open a web page that provides instant access to our comprehensive collection of free resources.

2

THE PROBLEM WITH TRADITION

The Illusion of Medical Infallibility

Our relationship with Anna didn't begin with soft lullabies and gentle cooing. It started with a battle—a clash with a system that demands obedience, even when obedience doesn't make sense. She had only just come into our home, we were her foster parents in the process of adopting her and were full of hope, promise and fear. And immediately, the system began to push against our instincts.

We've all been taught to see doctors as these all-knowing beings in white coats. We take their words as gospel truth. But let's be real; medicine isn't perfect. I already briefly mentioned how the medical establishment got smoking wrong, frontal lobotomies for mental illness wrong and even bioidentical hormones wrong. There are many books written on the topic of the history of medicine's blind spots.

But for me as a medical professional and new dad, Anna's case really put these limitations in stark relief. The traditional medical system set the bar so low for her, it was ridiculous. Her doctors said she wouldn't see, walk or talk. Even her other therapists (who genuinely cared for her) didn't have or offer much hope—they too were maintaining the status quo. But Anna had other plans.

The experts were dead wrong about Anna. And if they were wrong about her, they are likely wrong about many other patients. That realization lit a fire under me to challenge the medical status quo. We realized that to save Anna, we had to fight not just her illness, but an entire system that relied on antiquated ideas that had a chokehold on every unique patient's ability to heal. The traditional ways of prescribing one-size-fits-all procedures were holding our daughter back from reaching her potential, and we were willing to challenge it every way we had to.

When Standard Care Becomes Subpar

Remember that cute little smile I mentioned? Well, it almost disappeared forever, thanks to a feeding tube that no one questioned. At one of Anna's GI visits, the doctor said she was too small. The technical term for this is "failure to thrive." Her doctor's solution and the standard procedure? Put a tube in her stomach to pump in sugar-laden formula. They didn't care what kind of weight she gained or if the formula had any real nutrition. They just wanted to move her up the growth chart and call it a success story.

But something about the prescription and procedure felt off to me. My wife, Becky, is an occupational therapist. She explained to me that chewing and swallowing weren't just about eating—they were crucial for speech development and brain function. Kids who skipped this process often had long-term communication problems and higher risks of acid reflux and pneumonia ("Pediatric Feeding and Swallowing," University of Alabama, 2025). Also, the feeding tube would affect her ability to crawl, and crawling is a developmental precursor to walking ("Effects of Crawling Before Walking," Cazorla-González et al., 2022). It's a developmental milestone that every parent looks forward to. And Anna *was* eating—slowly, yes—but eating. Growing in her own time. We were feeding her. Loving her.

She was already healing. And everything in our gut screamed—this procedure isn't right.

According to doctors, she was never supposed to walk or crawl anyway, so that probably wasn't a concern for them. But we had higher hopes for her, and any procedure or recommendation that would create more limitations was worth questioning. In hindsight, as her parents, our response seemed natural, logical and inevitable. Why would we want to create more obstacles and limitations for a little girl already facing so many health challenges?

We said no to the feeding tube. And boy, did the system not like that.

The Day We Were Reported for Feeding Our Daughter Real Food

Rejecting the feeding tube procedure was really the beginning of our rebellion. The top pediatric GI specialist was livid. She wasn't used to being questioned—especially not by another physician, and certainly not by the occupational therapist sitting across from her (who also happened to be my wife). It didn't matter that Becky routinely worked with patients from her office, was familiar with the procedure and protocols and had been treating some of the toughest pediatric cases in the region. The moment we challenged this doctor's recommendation, the temperature in the room changed. She became dismissive, even harsh—especially toward Becky, who dared to challenge the so-called standard of care. And how did this physician—sworn under the Hippocratic Oath to first do no harm—respond to being challenged?

She called Child Protective Services.

That's right. Becky received a phone call days later. A nurse assigned to investigate potential abuse cases in our area was now opening an investigation into *us*. Our family. Because we had refused to let them cut a hole into a 14-month-old's stomach and pour formula (basically sugar water) into her body, bypassing her ability to eat, chew, swallow and grow, we were being subjected to one of the most painful and disruptive procedures a family can endure.

What that GI doctor didn't know was that Becky had worked with this nurse before. For years, she had served the local special needs population, regularly collaborating with the very professionals now charged with investigating her. Thankfully, the nurse knew Becky's work. She also knew the GI doctor's reputation for overusing feeding tubes—so much so that other providers in the system had a nickname for the pattern: *"proceduralized care."*

Still, we had to jump through hoops. We met with a nutritionist. We followed the nurse's guidelines. We played a game of chicken with the system, and the system flinched. I was still in the military at the time, so I knew how to work within a rigid system. We did everything required to prove we weren't dangerous—we were just fiercely protective. We were choosing real food over sugar water. Choosing chewing and swallowing for brain development over medical convenience. Let that sink in. We were reported for child neglect because we chose to refuse a medical procedure and feed our future daughter real food instead of pumping her full of sugar water.

The Growth Chart That Changed Everything

Six months after the scary experience of being reported to CPS, Becky made a discovery that challenged the procedure we felt we were being forced into. She found a growth chart specifically for children with cerebral palsy ("Low Weight, Morbidity, and Mortality in Children With Cerebral Palsy," Brooks et al., 2011). And there, clear as day, Anna was in the 50th percentile. She was normal for children in her condition.

The specialist had either ignored this growth chart or didn't know it existed (Becky and I still debate that to this day—how would an expert not know about this chart, or worse, ignore it?). I like to give the doctor the benefit of the doubt, but my wife still thinks this negligence was intentional and cruel. But the point is clear: If the top pediatric GI doctor in our area didn't know something this basic, they were likely missing many other crucial details.

We were seeing a brutal truth: the system punishes those who won't toe the line. It threatens, it coerces, it labels you dangerous when you dare to think differently. And we started to ask—what about the average parent? The one who is not married to a pediatric occupational therapist? The one who didn't get military training in how to hold their ground under pressure? All the parents who don't have medical degrees?

Most say yes. They comply.

And the child? The child gets the tube.

But not Anna.

This experience served its purpose, though: It lit a fire inside me. I realized if I couldn't rely on the so-called experts to know a simple fact about a kid's growth chart, then I couldn't trust them to understand the deeper complexities of Anna's condition. It was up to me.

No one else was going to get up at 4 am to research cerebral palsy, autism, gene-based nutrition, crystal meth-induced neurological damage and brain healing for Anna except me. No one else was going to worry or stress after work hours and on weekends about the missing facts, additional tests or missing information in their knowledge base to apply to this particular patient. No one else was going to dedicate themselves to creating a personalized treatment approach to my daughter. That realization changed everything. That doctor had to be me!

Defying Medical Expectations

We weren't looking for an ordinary outcome for Anna. We were aiming for extraordinary results. And that meant doing things differently. Not just slightly alternative or merely functional—we had to approach Anna and her condition in an entirely novel, unprecedented way. We weren't aiming for modest gains or slow progress; we were searching for a response that hadn't been seen before—something transformative, something the system didn't even recognize as possible. And even to this day, I don't think it has been previously done, except in her case. And this reality is devastating.

In the current system, kids born with cerebral palsy face a future of surgeries, botox injections, nerve-cutting procedures and muscle relaxants. Anna was no different, and that was what the system offered. But I knew there had to be a better way. Through neuromuscular stimulation (NMS)—a simple, noninvasive technique widely used in Europe—we activated her muscles, triggered feedback loops in her brain and reduced her muscle tone naturally. I used orthomolecular medicine (targeted nutrients to address small gene typos called SNPs) to bypass gene defects that affected her metabolism and hyperbaric medicine to activate her genes and stem cells. After years of daily therapy, Anna, at 19 years old, has had *zero* surgeries. This is unheard of and just doesn't happen. By this age many kids with her diagnosis have had *dozens* of procedures. The recommended spinal surgery alone would have cost $400000—but a $300 device saved us from this. And guess who told me about this device? A patient!

But here's the most shocking part: *No specialists ever suggested NMS to us.* This therapy, used by elite athletes to build muscle strength, was entirely unknown or ignored by our doctors. Multiply Anna's story across every specialty and every condition, and you begin to see why the system isn't just broken—it's failing its patients.

The system told us Anna would never *see*. Now, she reads and texts. They said she'd never crawl. Now, she walks with assistance. They claimed she'd never talk. Now, she sings to her grandparents, sometimes hours a day. (On a side note, just this past week, Anna asked for singing lessons so she can improve her singing. This happened after she heard an opera singer and said to me, "I can do that!" I love this kid!)

Every step of Anna's progress flew in the face of medical predictions. But it wasn't magic—it was the result of questioning everything, tireless research and refusing to accept others' imposed limitations as final.

Breaking Free: Healing Beyond the System

For Anna, healing required more than just avoiding unnecessary treatments. It meant *daily therapy, diligent nutrition, strict avoidance of harmful foods and consistent supplementation.* She became the hero of her own journey—with a team built around her to help her succeed.

One of my earliest interventions with Anna focused on targeted nutrition to influence her genetic expression. Another word for this is "nutrigenomics," which is how nutrients talk to your genes.

Some people have what are called single nucleotide polymorphisms (SNPs). Think of these as tiny typos in your genetic code. These small variations can alter how efficiently your body produces certain enzymes, which in turn affects how well your body uses nutrients. Depending on the severity of the SNP, a person's nutrient processing could drop to 80 percent, 40 percent or even stop altogether. This means that even with a healthy diet, the body might not be able to use key nutrients effectively.

One well-known SNP is in the **MTHFR gene**. People with this genetic variation have a significantly increased need for *methylated folate* (also called methylfolate or methylated folic acid). Without enough of it, they may be at higher risk for neurological problems, autoimmune conditions, cardiovascular disease and more. This deficiency can also elevate levels of a compound called **homocysteine**, an organic acid that builds up when the body lacks certain B vitamins—especially methylfolate—and is associated with inflammation and chronic illness.

In short, nutrigenomics allows us to identify these genetic roadblocks and use personalized nutrition to support the body's unique needs.

With Anna, I used genetic testing to look for these SNPs. Once we identified them, I tailored her nutritional support to compensate for these genetic inefficiencies. This process involved targeted supplementation to bypass or support the affected pathways. The delivery method for these supplements was horrible-tasting smoothies that made even me cringe—yet she diligently consumed them daily without complaint. Then came a breakthrough moment when she was about four years old. She discovered she could swallow capsules, and just like that, she left those nasty smoothies behind forever. But the deeper significance here isn't just about supplements. It's that Anna had an entire

ecosystem supporting her—a family completely committed to her healing, professionals coordinating her care and advocates fighting for her
at every turn. This network created the secure foundation that allowed
her to make transitions when she was developmentally ready. Her
ability to shift from smoothies to capsules wasn't just a small convenience—it represented how a child, given proper support, can adapt
and progress in ways that surprise everyone, including their doctors.

This should be the norm, *not the exception*.

True health isn't just about managing symptoms. It's about
reducing toxin exposure, improving nutrition through whole foods
and reconnecting with nature's healing power. It's about seeing what
others don't see, hearing what others don't hear and taking a holistic
approach to medicine—mind, body and spirit. And it's about person-
alizing it and making it your own.

More for Anna

We really committed to thinking and acting outside of the box for
Anna. Any parent will go to the ends of the earth to help their child,
but when you have a child with special needs, you need to go to
extraordinary lengths. Our fierce, unconditional love for Anna as her
parents merged with my professional expertise and analytical
approach, and this has become a powerful toolkit. I leveraged my
medical literacy and networking to become a super-specialist. I
would talk to any specialist about our options—from alternative
medicine practitioners drawing from ancient Chinese medicine to
mainstream physicians using proven methods to determine if they
might benefit my child. I read endless articles, studies, theories,
unpublished data, experimental methods and clinical trials to find a
key that might unlock a path to better health and outcomes for Anna.
I sifted through hype and pseudoscience, traveled internationally to
visit medical centers and met with specialists to push the boundaries
and limitations of the traditional "standards of care" being offered.

As you're learning, this endeavor has been deeply personal,

professionally challenging and many times emotionally taxing. But beyond the scientific curiosity and ambition that drove my early medical career, my relentless drive was now fueled by my love for Anna.

You don't have to be an MD to find novel approaches to treatment. But because I am, I now recognize this as a unique advantage and profound privilege. What good am I contributing to the field of medicine or my patients if my research, trials and findings only help my child and family?

This book is not about revealing a secret cure; it's about how my family had to look through a different lens to support *all of our* health to help us all achieve our maximum potential—beginning with Anna. But I want to give you a glimpse into some of the therapies we used and do it in a way that shows you there are options out there you and your doctor likely have not heard of before, and I want to do it in a way that is clear and makes sense.

But before I go through the list of therapies, I need to clarify one important thing: All of these treatments are built on solid foundations. If you don't get the foundations right, then all the high-tech, cool biohacking interventions won't work as well. Keep that in mind. Just like a professional athlete must perfect the basics, all the following therapies are built on top of these fundamentals. So you may ask, what are the basics? Here they are:

1. Eating Real Food

If you don't give your body the building blocks of real, sound nutrition, it's difficult for it to self-heal and self-repair.

2. Cultivating a Clean Environment

We must remove toxins and chemicals from our food and environment. This includes pesticides, petroleum products, cleaning chemicals and toxin-filled yard care products—everything. (If you want a comprehensive overview of this topic, check out our blog post on detoxification on our website: **AaronHartmanMD.com**.)

3. Physical Activity and Exercise

Because Anna couldn't walk, we had to develop specialized approaches to help her move (which are outlined below). These included therapies like suit therapy and electrical stimulation. The fundamental concept is simple: You must activate your body to move physically in order for everything else in your body to function appropriately.

4. Social Support Structures

For adults, this typically means having a sense of purpose and meaning in your life. For children, this means parents must provide a healthy family environment where they can thrive—one that helps them develop the ability to self-regulate their emotions and mood. You cannot underestimate the power of strong family and community connections in your body's path to healing.

You may wonder why I had to go to such extremes with both the holistic foundations and the high-tech medical stuff. The reason is because of Anna's specific condition. It was so dire that it required not just *perfection* of the foundations but a deep dive into all the science. For about 80 percent of the people I see, mastering the foundations listed above is sufficient to see improvements. But the really challenging cases and diagnoses require a deep dive into science and research. So below, you'll see that I'm sharing part of our personal *deep dive* into Anna's personalized medicine plan that we developed over the last 18 years.

Here's our roadmap of some of the therapies we've tried and continue to use with Anna. I'm sharing this not as medical advice, but as inspiration for your own health detective work—showing you what's possible and what's out there to explore and discover.

Therapies We've Tried and Used for Anna

HBOT (hyperbaric oxygen therapy): A treatment where a patient breathes 100 percent oxygen inside a pressurized chamber, which increases the amount of oxygen in the bloodstream and tissues. This enhanced oxygen delivery can accelerate healing, fight infection, reduce swelling and promote the growth of new blood vessels.

NMS (neuromuscular stimulation)—whole body and tone directed: This therapeutic technique uses electrical impulses to stimulate muscles and nerves, causing them to contract. It's used to strengthen muscles, increase range of motion and improve blood flow.

PEMF (pulsed electromagnetic field therapy) and pelvic PEMF: A noninvasive treatment that uses electromagnetic fields to stimulate the body's natural healing processes. It involves emitting low-frequency electromagnetic pulses that penetrate deep into tissues and cells, aiming to enhance cellular function and promote overall well-being.

TMS (transcranial magnetic stimulation): This noninvasive procedure uses magnetic fields to stimulate nerve cells in the brain. TMS works by delivering magnetic pulses to specific brain areas, typically the dorsolateral prefrontal cortex (DLPFC), which is involved in mood regulation.

tDCS (transcranial direct current stimulation): This is a noninvasive brain stimulation technique that uses weak electrical currents to modulate neuronal activity. It involves placing electrodes on the scalp, typically over a specific brain region of interest, and applying a low-intensity direct current. This stimulation can either increase or decrease the excitability of neurons in the targeted area.

TASES (task-specific electrical stimulation): This therapeutic technique uses electrical impulses to activate muscles during the performance of specific tasks or movements. It's designed to improve motor function, enhance muscle activation and facilitate motor learning by delivering stimulation in sync with a patient's attempted movements.

Peptides (Cerebrolysin, BPC 157, CJC/Ipa, TB4, TA1, Dihexa, Selank/Semax): The peptides we use help stimulate brain repair mechanisms, promote tissue healing and muscle growth and repair, reduce inflammation and enhance immune function.

Stem cells/exosomes: Stem cells and exosomes are both involved in regenerative therapies. Stem cells are actual cells with a nucleus that can replicate and differentiate into various cell types. Exosomes carry proteins, lipids and nucleic acids. Both stem cells and exosomes play a significant role in wound healing by promoting tissue regeneration and modulating the healing process.

Suit therapy/intensive longitudinal PT: Suit therapy is the use of specialized suits (like the TheraSuit or NeuroSuit) as a component of intensive rehabilitation (ILPT). This therapy emphasizes frequent and extended sessions allowing for faster skill-building, building muscle memory and strengthening neural pathways for quicker progress.

Galileo alternating therapy: This form of whole body vibration (WBV) therapy utilizes a side-alternating vibration platform to mimic the natural movement pattern of human walking. It helps with healing and rehab by activating and strengthening muscles. It triggers the stretch reflex, which leads to rhythmic, involuntary muscle contractions that benefit people with muscle weakness and neurological conditions that affect motor control.

Portable oral neural stimulation (PoNS): This device is a noninvasive treatment method that promotes healing and recovery for people with neurological conditions (including MS and traumatic brain injuries). The PoNS delivers mild electrical pulses to the tongue, which activates cranial nerves, stimulates neural impulses to the brainstem and cerebellum (key areas for motor control, balance and coordination) and promotes neuroplasticity.

eXciteOSA oral stimulation: This is a daytime oral device that uses neuromuscular electrical stimulation to target and strengthen the muscles of the tongue and upper airway. It improves muscle function and helps with sleep apnea, reduces snoring and improves sleep quality.

Low-level laser therapy (LLLT): This method is also known as cold laser therapy and promotes healing by stimulating cellular activity and reducing inflammation. By emitting low-intensity lasers or light-emitting diodes (LEDs), LLLT delivers light energy to cells, penetrating the skin and targeting cells—encouraging repair, reducing pain and alleviating inflammation.

Neuronic/brain-based low-level laser therapy (LLLT): Also referred to as photobiomodulation (PBM) or cold laser therapy, this method involves low-power lasers or LEDs to deliver specific wavelengths of light to the body, stimulating cellular activity and promoting healing. This is a noninvasive treatment that focuses on delivering the optimal amount of energy to cells, stimulating and enhancing cell function. It reduces inflammation, stimulates tissue repair and enhances blood flow and circulation.

Far infrared (FAR-IR): This is a specific wavelength of infrared radiation that can promote healing by increasing blood circulation, reducing inflammation and enhancing cellular repair. It achieves this by penetrating the body and stimulating cells, leading to improved oxygen and nutrient delivery to tissues, which is crucial for the healing process.

Visual therapy: This helps with healing by retraining the brain and eyes to work together more effectively, improving visual skills and alleviating visual symptoms. It addresses issues like poor eye teaming, focusing problems and difficulty with eye tracking—which can hinder daily activities. By improving the communication between the brain and eyes, vision therapy can improve visual performance, reduce strain and enhance overall quality of life.

Nicotinamide adenine dinucleotide (NAD+) IV: This therapy helps turn nutrients into usable energy so the body can fix damaged tissues quickly and safely. It aids in forming new cells and helps repair damaged cells, which is especially beneficial for recovering from injuries or surgeries since it can help speed up the healing process.

Methylene blue, low-dose naltrexone (LDN): Methylene blue, also known as methylthioninium chloride, was originally developed in 1876 as a synthetic, vibrant, cobalt blue colored dye for the textile industry. Its FDA-approved use is for treating methemoglobinemia, a rare blood condition that affects the blood's ability to carry oxygen. Methylene blue helps restore the oxygen-carrying capacity of red blood cells. New off-label uses include as a diagnostic aid, treatment for diseases like malaria, neuroprotective benefits (such as improving memory and cognitive function) and as a biofilm disrupter in chronic infections. Studies have shown synergistic benefits when combined with LDN, effectively targeting inflammation and modulating immune responses, addressing complex health conditions.

Small nucleotide polymorphism (SNP)-directed nutraceutical therapy: Also known as nutrigenomics or nutrigenetics, SNP explores how genetic variations influence an individual's response to nutrients and how tailoring nutrition based on these variations can promote healing and overall health. This therapy targets inflammation, optimizes nutrient metabolism and absorption, supports detox pathways and enhances immune function.

Oral and IV lipid therapy: This treatment addresses various issues related to cellular damage, drug toxicity and metabolic dysfunction. Lipid emulsions, often used in cases of local anesthetic systemic toxicity (LAST) and drug overdoses, can improve cardiac function and potentially impact cellular energy metabolism.

Epigenetic gene-directed detox therapy (EGDDT): Epigenetics is the study of how environmental factors influence gene expression to enhance the body's natural detoxification and healing processes. EGDDT is an approach that targets detoxification pathways, supports tissue repair and regeneration, combats inflammation and promotes cellular health. Interestingly, it also addresses addiction-related issues by changing the gene expression in the brain related to reward and craving.

Organic acid analysis and therapy: This treatment focuses on identifying and correcting imbalances in the body's metabolic pathways by measuring the levels of organic acids in urine. Organic acids are byproducts of cellular metabolism and can provide insights into various physiological processes—including energy production, neurotransmitter function, nutrient metabolism and detoxification pathways. Ultimately, this analysis uncovers underlying health issues and can help practitioners guide personalized treatment plans that target specific symptoms and their causes.

Advanced nutritional testing and therapy: This testing can play a significant role in promoting healing by addressing the root causes of health issues, helping us optimize nutrient intake to support the body's natural restorative processes and optimize gut health.

Advanced stool analysis: This diagnostic tool plays a crucial role in promoting gut healing by offering a comprehensive understanding of your digestive system's intricate ecosystem. It provides valuable information that goes beyond what standard tests offer, empowering you and your healthcare provider to develop targeted strategies for restoring gut health and improving overall well-being.

Heavy metal testing (HMT): Testing helps identify heavy metal accumulation before symptoms become severe or damage becomes irreversible. This allows early intervention and can prevent the development or progression of chronic illness (such as neurological, cardiovascular and autoimmune diseases).

Plasmalogen testing and therapy: Plasmalogens are specialized lipids crucial for maintaining the structure and function of cell membranes, particularly in the brain, heart and immune system. They play an important role in various bodily functions, including nerve activity, cell signaling and protection against oxidative stress. Plasmalogen testing allows for identifying nutritional deficiencies that can contribute to symptoms associated with neurodegenerative, inflammatory and cardiometabolic conditions.

Advanced metabolomic-directed nutraceuticals: This treatment helps with healing by addressing specific metabolic imbalances. It allows for detailed analysis of your unique metabolic profile so you can tailor interventions and treatment. It also targets key biomarkers, providing a more precise and effective approach to healing through nutritional optimization.

The Power of Parental Instinct

One of the most important lessons I learned through Anna's journey is how powerful a parent's gut feeling can be. As parents, we have this innate understanding of our kids that no amount of medical training can match. When the doctors pushed for a feeding tube for Anna, it was our parental instinct that told us it wasn't the right move. When they said she'd never walk or talk, it was our instinct that pushed us to keep trying and to keep believing in her potential.

This doesn't mean we should ignore medical advice completely! But it does mean we should trust our gut when something feels off—and science is just beginning to study the value of parental instinct ("Parental Intuition: A Phenomenological Structure of Intuitive Knowing in the Context of Child Illness and Shared Decision-Making in Healthcare," Shaw et al., 2025). It means we should feel empowered to ask questions, seek second opinions and fight tirelessly for our kids' well-being. And it means that we should not go through with medical treatments or surgery just because the expert says so.

A little aside here about my mother. She likes to keep me honest. When I tell her I'm an expert, even to this day, she likes to remind me what an expert is. "An 'ex' is a has-been and a 'spurt' is a little squirt of water." That's my mom for you. But you get the point.

I'm going to admit something here I probably shouldn't. I used to make fun of my mom when I was a kid. She would say some pretty "out there" things. For instance, "Cranberries are good for your blood because they are red...walnuts are good for your brain because they look like little brains." Pretty out-there stuff. However, what I've learned in the last 10 years is that walnuts are rich in alpha-linoleic acid and polyphenols, both great for the brain. Newer research has linked walnut consumption to improved memory and delayed cognitive decline ("Longer-Term Mixed Nut Consumption Improves Brain Vascular Function and Memory," Nijssen et al., 2023). And cranberries are particularly high in A-type proanthocyanidins, which help improve cardiovascular health by preventing the oxidation of LDL cholesterol ("Low-Calorie Cranberry Juice Supplementation Reduces Plasma Oxidized LDL and Cell Adhesion Molecule Concentrations in Men," Ruel et al., 2008). How did my mom intuitively know this?

The Myth of the All-Knowing Doctor

Doctors don't have all the answers. They're human beings doing their best with the knowledge they have. But that knowledge base is always changing, and no single person can keep up with every new development in medicine. Some doctors continue their education and approach their practice with curiosity and an open mind. But not all.

When we put doctors on pedestals expecting them to be perfect practitioners who have all the answers, we set ourselves up for disappointment. More importantly, we miss out on the chance to be active participants in our own healthcare. Instead of viewing doctors as infallible authorities, think of them as partners in your health journey. They bring valuable expertise to the table, but so do you. You know your body, your child and your symptoms better than anyone else. That knowledge is invaluable in the diagnostic and treatment process.

Remember, I'm saying this as a doctor! My training and early years as a practitioner were based on the old, traditional ways of treating patients. Some traditions are great: opening presents on Christmas morning, celebrating birthdays and summer trips to the beach. But when doing things the traditional way is causing harm, it's time to revisit the way we do things: When we know better, we do better.

I get it; challenging medical authority isn't easy—even if you are a medical professional like me. It can be scary to question a doctor who has years of training and experience, who is an expert in their field and specialization. But remember, you're not challenging their expertise—you're asking them to listen to your expertise about yourself, your child or your loved one. You are requesting that they look at your unique situation more closely and differently than from all the other patients they have seen. There has been a radical shift in the practice of medicine since I started my training back in 1996. Back then, I was told that evidence-based medicine included the clinical expertise of the practicing physician ("Evidence Based Medicine: What It Is and What It Isn't," Sackett et al., 1996). Today, it almost entirely relies on randomized trials. The problem with this approach is that you cannot individualize these trials to the person in front of you. The result is a medical-industrial complex that treats patients like widgets to churn out results, often overlooking the nuances that a personalized precision approach would give. More on this later.

When we rejected the feeding tube for Anna, we weren't saying the doctor was wrong about everything. We were saying that this particular solution didn't feel right for our child. And guess what? That decision led to better outcomes for Anna.

Challenging authority doesn't mean being combative or disrespectful. It means asking thoughtful questions, doing your own research and being an active participant in your healthcare decisions. If your doctor dismisses your requests, concerns or questions—find another doctor. Some doctors don't like questions. That's their problem, not yours. Remember this: You have every right to be part of your care. If a doctor can't handle your questions, it might be time for a new one. Look for providers who welcome teamwork. They exist, and they can change your healthcare experience. Building a team of open-minded practitioners is like creating your own health squad. It can make a huge difference.

If there's one thing I want you to take away from this chapter, it's this: You have to take ownership of your own health. The system doesn't always have your best interests in mind—it's often not designed to support individualized treatment plans; instead it's buttressed by the status quo. It's up to you to be your own advocate— or your child's—in the face of medical challenges.

This doesn't mean you have to become a medical expert overnight. It means staying informed, asking questions, seeking second opinions when necessary and trusting your instincts when something doesn't feel right. All you are asking for is to understand your diagnosis and treatment options. But you have to take owner-ship of the decisions being made.

Remember Anna's story. If we had blindly followed every piece of medical advice we received, she wouldn't be where she is today. It was our willingness to challenge the system, to seek out alternative approaches, maintain curiosity and to never give up that led to her extraordinary progress.

The Road Ahead: Embracing a New Approach to Healthcare

As we move forward, we need to rethink our approach to healthcare. We need a collaborative system that values patient input, that sees individuals rather than just symptoms and that's willing to admit when it doesn't have all the answers.

This shift starts with us. By becoming informed patients, asking questions and challenging assumptions when necessary, we can push the healthcare system to be better. We can encourage a more collabo-rative approach to medicine, where doctors and patients work together as partners.

Anna's journey taught me that miracles don't just happen by acci-dent—we are a crucial part of making them happen. By refusing to accept limitations, by questioning the status quo and by never giving up hope, we can achieve outcomes that defy all expectations. But it will be an uphill battle, so get in shape and get ready for the climb.

As her parents, we said no to feeding tubes, surgeries and a hospi-talization that Anna didn't need, as well as to treatments that could hurt her. We fought back when they tried to put Anna in a box. And that fight changed us forever. The system is not all bad, but it needs to work better for those it is supposed to be caring for.

Facing the system and standing your ground is where lives change. Where parents become fighters. Where patients become advocates. Where hope finds a way, even when things are really dark. It's real. It's tough. And it will change how you deal with doctors, hospitals and the healthcare system at large.

Here's my challenge to you: The next time you're faced with a

medical decision, don't just nod and accept your doctor's recommendation. Ask questions. Do your research. Trust your instincts.
Because if Anna's story proves anything, it's that the most powerful
force in healthcare isn't a doctor's expertise or a cutting-edge treatment—it's the unwavering determination of someone who refuses to
give up.

Remember, if Anna can defy every expectation, so can you. Let's
challenge the system together, and in doing so, open up a world of
possibilities for ourselves and our loved ones. But first, let's get into
the nitty-gritty of the system as it stands today—I'm going to reveal
even more about the flaws in the healthcare system and how even the
smartest doctors are missing the obvious in the way they practice medicine.

SCAN THE **QR** code below with your phone's camera. This will direct you to open a web page that provides instant access to our comprehensive collection of free resources.

3

BLIND SPOTS

Our current healthcare system is failing all of us. It didn't just fail my daughter. It has failed every patient who walks into my clinic today. That's why they come to see me! A typical patient I see has been to multiple specialists—sometimes even at major university medical centers. They have a litany of "unrelated symptoms" that, to date, no other medical doctor has been able to adequately interpret and address. And they've been told one of three things:

- There's nothing wrong with them.
- They can't be helped (with their autoimmune, inflammatory, gut or neurological condition).
- Or worst of all: *It's all in your head.*

They are gaslit, made to believe their suffering is just anxiety or stress. And then, exhausted and desperate, they come to me. I listen. I connect the dots.

I'd like to introduce you to one of my patients, Sarah. She's 35, works in marketing and thought she was doing everything right— eating well, exercising and getting regular checkups. But then, out of nowhere, she started feeling awful. Her symptoms were extreme fatigue, brain fog and aches all over her body. Her doctors ran tests. They gave her medications. But nothing helped—in fact, she felt worse.

Sarah isn't an anomaly. She's a typical patient that comes to my clinic—and this should be a wake-up call for the entire medical community. Even with all our advanced medicine, treatments, studies, research, medication options and expertise, there are still massive blind spots. Patients for whom the system simply doesn't work. Where people like Sarah slip through the cracks.

So what was my diagnosis? What was the root cause of Sarah's illness?

It wasn't just random bad luck. It was something deeper. Something that conventional medicine overlooked—nutrient deficiencies, toxins in her environment or maybe the mold exposure from her college dorm. It could have been chronic stress or an undiagnosed gut issue.

But no one bothered to check.

I spent over two hours talking to Sarah about her symptoms, her environment, her lifestyle and her habits (in my office, the initial intake visit is two to two and a half hours). After our visit, I uncovered the real culprits behind her struggles—ongoing mold exposure in her home and chronic gut dysfunction. Advanced stool testing and inflammatory markers revealed she had small intestinal bacterial overgrowth (SIBO) and chronic inflammatory response syndrome (CIRS)—both triggered by mold exposure in her home.

By healing her gut and removing her from the toxic environment, everything changed. Her symptoms faded, her health rebounded and the following year, she and her husband's dream finally came true—she got pregnant.

Stories like Sarah's aren't rare for me. I see them routinely—patients who are overlooked by the system and who finally find hope and healing when we dare to look deeper. I will go more in depth into Sarah's diagnosis and recovery later.

The Gut: The Blind Spot That Took 4500 Years to Recognize

It's mind-blowing to think that even in the year 2024, mainstream medicine laughed at the idea of a "leaky gut" or the gut being linked to chronic illness (leaky gut, also called increased intestinal permeability, is a condition where the lining of the small intestine becomes more permeable than normal, allowing substances like bacteria and toxins to pass into the bloodstream ["Intestinal Permeability Disturbances: Causes, Diseases and Therapy," Macura et al., 2024]). As of this writing, McGill University (also known as the "Harvard of Canada") still thinks this is not scientific and is more of an *Alice in Wonderland* phenomena ("You Probably Don't Have Leaky Gut," Jarry, 2024). Yet, traditional Chinese medicine recognized this over 4500 years ago, teaching that "death begins in the bowels." Ayurvedic medicine from India said the same. Even Hippocrates, the father of modern medicine, stated in the fifth century B.C. that "death begins in the gut." For decades, conventional medicine ignored these ancient truths and ridiculed those who treated leaky gut as unscientific quacks.

But I would say that gut health is finally gaining recognition as the root cause of countless health conditions in many medical communities ("Intestinal Permeability Disturbances: Causes, Diseases and Therapy," Macura et al., 2024). Yet somehow, despite our understanding of the diet and digestion link and the popularity of alternative treatment methods, our current healthcare system still lacks the tools to properly address our problems with gut health. Even today, GI doctors in my local community dismiss concepts like dysbiosis (an imbalance in the composition or function of the gut's natural bacteria, fungi and viruses) and leaky gut as pseudoscience. But can I really blame the medical community? Insurance doesn't cover the necessary testing. Gut health is not featured in the medical journals (all publications that are heavily influenced by pharmaceutical advertising). And as specialists, their compensation is tied to performing procedures, not spending time investigating root causes of disease and symptoms with their patients. In reality, the system itself dictates how medical care is delivered, prioritizing interventions over true healing.

There's no prescription drug for healing a damaged gut.

No one-size-fits-all antibiotic to fix gut permeability.

So the system pretends that gut health is not a real problem—or it just ignores it as a problem until a pharmaceutical company creates a drug to "treat" it. It's backwards, upside down and inside out.

More Missing Pieces in Medicine

When I first saw Sarah and ran lab tests on her, she also had positive thyroid antibodies, leading to a diagnosis of Hashimoto's thyroiditis. No other medical doctor had bothered to do that testing on her either —even though autoimmune thyroid issues are incredibly common. And she's not alone. Roughly 38 percent of women and 30 percent of men in the United States have a positive autoantibody, meaning they're already on the path toward autoimmune disease but just don't know it yet ("Autoantibodies Associated With Connective Tissue Diseases," Didier et al., 2018). So why isn't our system screening for this? Because unless the symptoms are screaming and meet a diagnostic checkbox, the system does nothing. No diagnosis. No treatment. Just watchful waiting—while the disease progresses quietly beneath the surface.

Autoimmune diseases don't just happen—they follow a pattern. By definition, four key factors must be present (*Vaccines and Autoimmunity,* Shoenfeld et al., Wiley-Blackwell, 2015):

1. A genetic predisposition
2. A triggering event
3. Increased gut permeability (*remember, the thing that "doesn't exist"*)
4. A chronic infection or colonization

For Sarah, two of these were leaky gut and an underlying chronic infection—her SIBO. Addressing these didn't just help her feel better;

it also halted the progression of her previously undiagnosed autoimmune condition.

Yet conventional medicine rarely looks at these root causes. These factors are often ignored—unless a patient finds their way to a functional medicine clinic.

The Silent Epidemic Lurking in Plain Sight: Sleep Deprivation

Our healthcare system continues to overlook one of the most fundamental pillars of health—sleep. Yet sleep deprivation remains a silent epidemic, quietly affecting millions without the attention it deserves.

The average American today sleeps about six hours per night ("Are Americans Sleeping Less Than They Used To?," Lauderdale, 2015). Just 150 years ago, we averaged eight and a half hours per night (CDC, 2024). Medical experts know that sleep is medicine for the brain—a time for healing, immune restoration and cellular repair. And yet most of us are *chronically* sleep-deprived.

School schedules force kids to wake up too early. College students are exhausted. The average adult has lost 25 percent of their sleep compared to previous generations. This isn't just a personal problem —it's a missing diagnosis. A blind spot in our healthcare system. Despite mountains of research linking poor sleep to everything from metabolic disorders to cognitive decline, most doctors barely ask about it.

No one is screening for chronic sleep deprivation. There's no routine sleep assessment during annual checkups. Instead, patients who complain of fatigue are handed prescriptions for stimulants, sleep aids, antidepressants or are told it's just stress.

Quick side note here. There was a big push to treat insomnia (a particular type of loss of sleep) in the 1990s when Ambien first came to the market. It took about 15 years to discover that chronic Ambien use actually increases all-cause mortality (i.e., *dying for any reason*) and other medications used for sleep adversely affect memory, increase the risk of falling and actually don't improve sleep quality

("Effect of Anxiolytic and Hypnotic Drug Prescriptions on Mortality Hazards: Retrospective Cohort Study," Scott et al., 2014). The side effects became so well-known that there was even a TV episode of *CSI* in which Ambien use was part of the crime scene. That short burst of medical interest in treating insomnia has since puttered out.

But the impact of lost sleep is massive. It weakens the immune system, disrupts hormones and accelerates aging ("Sleep, Sleep Disorders and Immune Function," Tan et al., 2019). It's a root cause of chronic disease that most of the medical world completely ignores ("Poor Sleep Alters Immune Cells, Increasing Risk for Inflammatory Diseases," Lam, 2025). And yet, it's one of the easiest causes of poor health to fix (from a functional medicine perspective)—if only the system recognized it as a real problem.

This is just one more example of how modern medicine overlooks the most basic foundations of health. Another blind spot. If we truly want to heal, we need to start addressing the blind spots that are hiding in plain sight.

The Problem With Our Healthcare System

Our healthcare system does not have answers for many health problems. Think about that for a moment. Then consider the following: The system *still* functions the same way it did for my grandfather in the 1950s and 1960s. It's based on an outdated model:

1. You develop an acute illness.
2. You see a doctor.
3. They diagnose you in one visit.
4. They prescribe medication.
5. You move on.

This model worked when strep throat used to cause heart disease, tuberculosis was commonplace, a cancer diagnosis was a certain death sentence and surgical procedures were life-threatening—when something as simple as removing an appendix could kill you. Medicine was revolutionized by hand washing, clean water, advanced surgical procedures, antibiotics and vaccinations. Now, chronic diseases like heart disease and cancer are the most common causes of death in the US, not infections (like it was in my grandfather's time) (CDC, 2024). And medical errors, which we will discuss later, are the third most common cause of death in our country. Unbelievable, I know. Just suspend your disbelief for a few chapters and be ready to have your mind blown!

But we are still practicing medicine today as if we're stuck in that era.

It's time for an upgrade.

We need a new way to look at health.

A new way to understand the complex systems of the human body.

A new way to help the body do what it was designed to do: *self-heal and self-repair.*

Failure Isn't an Option

Every story has a hero and a villain. In my family's story, the antagonist wasn't one person—it was the entire system. It's not that there were insufficient treatment options, it's that we weren't receiving adequate treatment. These included:

- The GI doctor who wanted to cut a hole in my daughter's stomach because they misdiagnosed her slow growth as "failure to thrive."
- The orthopedic surgeon who wanted to cut her heel cords because that was the only option they had for her feet to fully touch the floor.
- The second opinion we sought from another institution after refusing to cut her heel cords—to install a baclofen pump into her back to treat her muscle spasticity (they couldn't decide which was best).

- The ophthalmologist who wanted to cut her eye muscles because that was the standard of care for her eye condition.
- The physiatrist who wanted to cut parts of her spinal cord nerves in a procedure known as dorsal rhizotomy.

We fought against this system. We struggled. And ultimately, we overcame it. If the saying is "Fool me once, shame on you. Fool me twice, shame on me," categorize me as someone who refused to be fooled at all. When it came to my daughter, the consequences of failure were just too great. And my fight for her inspired and informed my fight for my patients.

This journey to find the right treatment plan for Anna changed how I practiced medicine for my patients. Doctors are trained to believe they have all the answers—that we are the experts and know everything. But I've learned an undeniable truth: Patients have *invaluable* insights, experience and their own expertise.

A patient in one of our first online communities introduced me to a neuromuscular stimulation device, Revitive, that transformed my daughter's muscle tone. I had never heard of it before, but after using it for six months, most of the tension in my daughter's calves and hamstring muscles was gone and she could stand up straight without assistance. No surgery specialist could promise me this dramatic outcome. But if I had dismissed her suggestion because she wasn't an "expert," I never would have tried it with my daughter. Five years later, Anna still uses Revitive every day. It has profoundly impacted her leg tone, calf strength and ability to stand.

So the failure in healthcare is not just because of shortcomings in the system, and it's not just the blind spots in medical care. We are also failing because we aren't listening to the patients we are supposed to be caring for.

Your Turn: Spotting Your Blind Spots

Now, it's time to take action.

Grab a notebook. Write down three times you dealt with the healthcare system—good or bad. For each one, ask yourself:

How did I feel?
What worked?
What didn't?
Did they listen to all my concerns?
Did I feel heard?
Did I later find out something was missed, overlooked,
ignored or I figured it out on my own?

This simple act of asking yourself how the care you are receiving makes you feel reveals patterns you may have missed. Maybe you always feel rushed. Maybe you never question your doctor's recommendations. Maybe you've been given medications without anyone asking *why* you got sick in the first place, and what if you are prescribed something in error? What if your doctor makes a mistake? The stakes are too great for you not to be involved in your own healthcare.

Once you identify these blind spots, you can start asking better questions of your providers—questions that will help you take charge of your health.

The Future of Healthcare Starts With You

Hippocrates once said, "It is more important to know what sort of person has a disease than to know what sort of disease a person has."

Your health is more than just symptoms. It's your body, mind, environment and experiences.

By learning to recognize and address healthcare's blind spots, you become an *active participant* in your healing—a collaborator in your care.

You develop the confidence to demand care that sees all of you—not just your symptoms. In doing so, you unlock your health potential and feel better than you ever thought possible. Your journey to better health starts now. It's time to see beyond the blind spots. But where do you start? Let's go with the gut.

Scan the QR code below with your phone's camera. This will direct you to open a web page that provides instant access to our comprehensive collection of free resources.

4

MEALS CAN HEAL

L ike so many pivotal changes in my life over the past 24 years, this journey began with my wife, Becky. She has always been the catalyst—whether bringing Anna into our lives, nudging me toward starting a functional medicine practice or challenging how we nourished our family. Becky has an uncanny ability to see the big picture before I do, and this time was no different.

It all started with a book: *Animal, Vegetable, Miracle* by Barbara Kingsolver. This story of a family living off the land, eating only what was available seasonally, fascinated Becky. Each family member allowed themselves one "cheat food," but otherwise, they committed to growing and sourcing food locally. One evening, as she closed the book, Becky turned to me and said, "Maybe we should consider doing something similar. Maybe we should get into eating real food."

At the time, I shrugged. It sounded intriguing, but frankly, I wasn't ready for a massive lifestyle overhaul. What I didn't realize was that this seemingly small conversation would alter the trajectory of our lives—and my medical practice—forever.

My Reluctant Start

IN 2008-2009, I wasn't thinking about food as medicine. I had not yet grasped Hippocrates' wisdom of "Let food be thy medicine," nor had I connected gut health to chronic illness. I saw food as fuel—nothing more.

I resisted at first. I liked my neatly manicured lawn and didn't want to give up weed preventers or insecticides. The thought of swapping out my favorite processed snacks for something "closer to the earth" didn't excite me. But Becky, persistent as ever, started making small shifts in our home. She swapped out prepackaged foods for fresh, local produce. She experimented with homemade sourdough bread. And slowly, despite my reluctance, I found myself coming along for the ride.

One moment stands out vividly. I was researching how environmental toxins affect health, and I stumbled upon something alarming: The very chemicals I was using to keep my lawn pristine—herbicides, pesticides and glyphosate (Roundup)—were deeply linked to chronic disease. Worse, these chemicals were likely affecting not just my health, but Anna's healing journey ("Effects of Glyphosate Exposure on Human Health: Insights from Epidemiological and in Vitro Studies," Agostini et al., 2020).

That realization hit me like a ton of bricks. What if my stubborn attachment to convenience and a pristine yard was making things worse for my daughter?

The Soil-Health Connection

Once we committed to this path, I became fascinated by compost and dirt. *Soil and Health* by Sir Albert Howard opened my eyes to something I had never considered: The quality of our soil directly influences human health. Howard observed this phenomenon nearly a century ago in India—healthy soil produced robust crops, and in turn, healthier animals and people. If the bacteria, pH balance and micronutrients in soil determined the vitality of plants, then it made perfect sense that our bodies—fueled by those plants—relied on that same balance.

This concept made me look differently at everything, from the food on our plates to the way we treated illness. And it led me down another rabbit hole—one that changed how we cared for our children.

My curiosity soon brought me to Weston A. Price, a dentist from the early 20th century whose personal tragedy turned into a global mission. He lost his son to a dental abscess. He couldn't fathom how, in such a modern age, a child could die from something so preventable—something that should never have been life-threatening in the first place. Fueled by grief and a relentless need for answers, he traveled the world studying isolated communities—from the Maasai in Africa to the Swiss in the Lötschental Valley. What he uncovered was striking: These communities, untouched by processed foods, had virtually no cavities or chronic illness. Their diets were rich in nutrient-dense animal products, high-vitamin butter, fermented foods and unrefined ingredients.

That resonated deeply—especially with Anna, who had been exposed to crystal meth in utero. Children in her situation often suffer from weak enamel and are prone to frequent dental issues. At first, I thought fluoride would help. I didn't just try it—I overdid it. I supplemented her with fluoride, believing it would protect her vulnerable teeth. Becky, however, already knew better. She warned me, gently but persistently, that fluoride could be harmful—that it was a known neurotoxin, linked to IQ reduction and abnormal teeth development ("Fluoride Exposure and Children's IQ Scores," Taylor, PhD et al., 2025; "Association Between Maternal Fluoride Exposure During Pregnancy and IQ Scores in Offspring in Canada," Green et al., 2019). I dismissed her concerns and went forward with it for a full year. Looking back, I can admit: not my finest parenting moment. But thankfully, she was patient and eventually I listened. Weston A. Price's work was an important part of that journey for me.

Remarkably, as of the writing of this chapter, the US Secretary of Health has recommended that the CDC reconsider fluoride levels in our drinking water. The reason? Emerging research links fluoride consumption with lowered IQ scores in children and identifies it as a potential endocrine disruptor affecting hormonal systems (National Research Council, 2006). Is this yet another blind spot in public health policy? It certainly appears so. While the scientific and regulatory communities are just beginning to acknowledge these concerns, our family made this connection and removed fluoride from our water supply 15 years ago—well ahead of official recognition. This pattern of institutional delay in responding to evidence is precisely what drives many families to take health matters into their own hands rather than waiting for consensus to catch up with reality.

After studying Price's tome *Nutrition and Physical Degeneration*, I learned about the healing power of nutrient-dense food—particularly high-vitamin butter and cod liver oil. We began using those with our children, and the results in our family were profound. Anna, now 19, has never had a cavity. Neither has our daughter Abigail. Khalil only developed cavities after forming a habit of drinking lemon juice through a straw. Once he stopped, the cavities stopped. But the benefits went far beyond teeth.

Anna has only been on antibiotics once since we've had her. That's it. Khalil and Abigail? Between the three of them, our children have needed antibiotics just twice in their entire lives. That's nearly unheard of today. It wasn't magic. It was food. It was the soil. It was learning to trust in nature's design and stepping away from synthetic "fixes" that only mask the real issues.

And this wasn't just about teeth—it was about the bigger picture. What if more families had access to this kind of information? What if we stopped viewing nutrition as supplementary and started seeing it as foundational? What began as curiosity turned into conviction, and that conviction changed the health of our entire family.

A quick note about my family: I don't talk much about my other two adopted children in this book—Abigail and Khalil. They both have equally amazing stories, having come from similarly hard places as Anna. But Anna's story is the most illustrative of how our lives and my career changed, so she became the thread that weaves through these pages. I want you to know, though, that Anna's remarkable outcomes aren't unique in our family. Both Abigail and Khalil have experienced similar transformations using these same principles. And as I write this today, thousands of patients in my practice have achieved results that once seemed impossible.

So while Anna's story anchors this book, she represents something much larger—proof that this approach works consistently, across different conditions, different ages and different starting points. Her journey isn't an anomaly; it's a blueprint.

But I'll let you be the judge of that!

From Nutrition to Farming

Eventually, we considered taking things a step further. What if we started our own homestead? I wanted to understand the entire food chain—because healthy cows produce healthy meat and milk, and to grow healthy cows, they need the right nutrition.

Enter Joel Salatin, the rebellious farmer and author of *Folks, This Ain't Normal*. His philosophy further cemented what I was learning: soil health dictates animal health, and in turn, human health. Our modern food system strips away vital nutrients, leaving us nutritionally bankrupt.

One of Salatin's stories that he told me in person stuck with me. Conventional cattle feed lacked critical trace minerals—iodine, selenium, magnesium—leading to weak cows plagued with chronic issues. When Salatin supplemented his cows with kelp, a natural trace mineral source, something remarkable happened: The cows' health transformed, infections disappeared and they no longer needed antibiotics.

This reminds me of a landmark study from China that revolutionized our understanding of viral-induced heart disease and selenium's protective role. While a US pharmaceutical company was developing an expensive vaccine to prevent the viral infection causing heart disease, researchers discovered something far simpler and more profound: Selenium deficiency was actually enabling the virus to mutate into more virulent forms ("An Original Discovery: Selenium Deficiency and Keshan Disease," Chen, 2012). Children who received basic selenium supplementation showed complete protection against the disease—their bodies naturally resisted the virus when properly nourished. The results were so definitive that the vaccine development was abandoned in favor of addressing the underlying nutritional deficiency. Instead, selenium was distributed throughout the affected regions, effectively eliminating a disease that conventional medicine had approached as a vaccination challenge rather than a nutritional one. This case perfectly illustrates a powerful principle: Small, targeted micronutrient interventions can have massive public health implications, often more effectively than complex medical interventions.

The Wisdom in Our Environment

As a result of our family's move to a farm, much of what we have learned about health didn't come from medical textbooks—it came from nature. Within the confines of our own family experience, we explored principles that shaped our understanding of true wellness.

Part of our journey was homesteading with our own farm animals. Great! But I realized I didn't want my cows dying, so I had to learn all I could about raising healthy cows. That meant diving deep into the principles of regenerative agriculture, studying the intricate relationship between soil microbes, forage quality and animal vitality. We learned how to raise our own food, understanding the deep connections between soil health, animal husbandry and human nutrition. Our children have thrived in this environment. They wanted to be outside, to push themselves harder, to engage with the world in a way that built resilience and grit. This took about two years of reading, hands-on research and trial and error—but the result has been thriving, healthy farm animals and a family more deeply connected to the source of their food.

One of our children became fascinated with mushrooms. He went foraging, studied them and uncovered their incredible benefits for immune health, cognitive function and overall vitality. That led us to other discoveries—raising our own chickens and learning how eggs rich in phospholipids are essential for brain and nervous system function. And guess what? Mainstream medicine is starting to catch up with what our family discovered over 15 years ago. This past year, a research article was published showing how healthy fats in eggs can prevent Alzheimer's disease. Eating just one egg a week can lower the risk for this disease by 47 percent, and an egg a day can lower the odds of dementia by 78 percent ("Association of Egg Intake With Alzheimer's Dementia Risk in Older Adults: The Rush Memory and Aging Project," Pan et al., 2024; "Association Between Egg Consumption and Dementia in Chinese Adults," Igbinigie et al., 2024)! Just another example of how the wisdom in nature that's been around for thousands of years is finally being discovered by modern medicine.

We started drinking raw milk, making homemade yogurt and kefir and only later did we realize how profoundly these fermented foods support gut health and immune function. I remember reading *Soil and Health* by Sir Albert Howard and having a breakthrough moment. The health of the soil dictates the health of the plants that grow in it, which dictates the health of the animals that eat the plants —and ultimately, of those who eat both: us. I had never heard of this in medical school yet this book was written in 1947. Over 75 years ago!

Then I learned something even more astonishing: When a breast-feeding mother pulls plants from her garden, then eats those plants, the bacteria on those plants transfer to her gut, then into her breast milk, directly influencing her baby's gut and immune system. You cannot make this up. The complexity is astounding. It's almost as if nature is *designed* to help us heal—if we just pay attention.

The Nutritional Deficiency Epidemic

All my research raised a burning question: Could our national health crisis be largely due to nutritional deficiencies ("Well Fed but Undernourished: An American Epidemic," Kresser, 2018)? The more I researched, the clearer it became:

- 50 percent of Americans do not get enough magnesium
  ("Half of Americans Do Not Get Enough Magnesium,"
  Allison, 2025).
- More than 90 percent are potassium deficient ("98 percent
  of American Diets Potassium Deficient," Greger, 2013).
- 20 to 40 percent have deficiencies in at least one B vitamin
  ("Factors Contributing to the High Prevalence of Vitamin
  B6 Deficiency in US," Tang et al., 2018).

Is this yet another blind spot in our current healthcare system? These deficiencies have devastating consequences—low magnesium and potassium contribute to high blood pressure, insulin resistance and diabetes. B-vitamin deficiencies are linked to neurological issues, fatigue and chronic disease ("Vitamin B12 Status: Are Genetics a Driving Factor?," Burhans, 2018).

Why? Because processed food has stripped away nearly everything our bodies need. When grains are refined, 80 percent of their nutrients vanish. The FDA mandates adding back a few synthetic B vitamins just to prevent diseases like pellagra (B3 deficiency) and beriberi (B1 deficiency), but it's still not enough (that's where the term "enriched" comes from in foods like conventional bread). Connecting these dots changed how I practiced medicine. More importantly, it profoundly shaped my children's health.

You've heard a lot about Anna, but let me introduce you to our son, Khalil. He also had a lot of early health challenges, and his story underscores everything we've learned about total health.

When we brought Khalil home at six months of age, he had debilitating asthma and eczema. Becky slept with him on her chest every night for the first week he was in our care, terrified he would stop breathing at night. His skin was covered in red, inflamed eczema patches.

He needed formula, but Becky refused commercial options filled with synthetic ingredients. Instead, she researched and made a homemade formula herself. Within two weeks, his breathing improved. Within six weeks, his skin cleared. Within a year, his asthma and eczema had disappeared. Today, at 14, he rarely wheezes and has never needed antibiotics or steroids for his asthma and eczema—ever! The only time he gets sick? After church camp, where he eats processed food (or has similar exposures).

The same is true for Anna—one round of antibiotics in 19 years. That's it. And Abigail? None!

The Final Piece: Collagen, Bone Broth and Connective Tissue

One of my later discoveries was the power of bone broth. Packed with collagen and trace minerals, it's a lost staple that once played a vital role in human health. Before the 1950s, a lot of meat consumption in the US came from organ meats—rich in these same trace nutrients. Today, hardly anyone eats organ meats, and bone broth has all but disappeared from our diets ("Why Don't Americans Eat Organ Meats?," Zhang, 2024). Could this be contributing to modern chronic illness? I believe so.

The Bigger Picture

A single book recommendation from Becky set all of this in motion. One small step led to a series of realizations, transformations and near-miraculous health changes for our children.

Today, I apply these principles in my clinic daily and continue to be amazed by the profound results in my patients. But as I dug deeper, another question emerged: *If the evidence is so clear, why aren't more doctors seeing this?* That's what we'll explore next—the broken medical education system that keeps doctors trapped in outdated thinking.

Becky put together an incredible resource that has transformed how our patients approach food—and I want you to have it. It distills my six core real food principles into a practical, easy-to-follow food sourcing guide. No matter where you live in the US, this guide will help you navigate the overwhelming world of food choices with confidence. It took our family *two years* to figure out how to source the cleanest, most nutrient-dense foods—this guide will fast-track that process for you. And the best part? You can share it with your family and friends, empowering them to take control of their health, too.

Also, I have a reading list on my website of over 70 books (**Aaron-HartmanMD.com**). I had over a thousand book recommendations given to me. I read over 400 of them and narrowed the list down to those that I think have the most value for patients. I've made this list readily available to the public. I'm not a gatekeeper! I want you to win. I know you have a lot of questions, and I'll answer a few of the most common ones in the next chapter.

Scan the QR code below with your phone's camera. This will direct you to open a web page that provides instant access to our comprehensive collection of free resources.

5

Q&A: NATURAL HEALING WITH NUTRITION

I n this chapter, I'm tackling all the most commonly asked questions that my patient community needs answered. If you've picked up this book, chances are you are seeking the same answers. Becoming a collaborator on your journey to total health requires a lot of changes and a commitment to yourself to make these changes. Remember: You aren't alone. Even with my medical training, I had the same questions! And my patient community is here for you, too.

Q: How do I handle the initial challenges of switching to a real food diet?

A: Look, changing your diet can feel like a lot at first. I get it. When Becky first read *Animal, Vegetable, Miracle,* it changed everything about how we looked at and interacted with food. But don't sweat it! Start small. Swap out one meal a day. Or start by removing "fake" foods from your home one at a time. What's "fake?" For example, start by removing all the processed oils—like canola and soy—for real whole-food oils like avocado and extra virgin olive oils.

Get creative in the kitchen. Get the kids involved in cooking—they're more likely to eat what they help make. When we started our shift to whole foods and total nutrition, we turned it into a game, trying a new veggie each week. It made our dramatic diet changes feel like a fun family adventure. Remember, it's all about baby steps. Every fake, processed food replaced with a real one is a win for your family's health.

Q: What if I'm struggling to find time for natural living in our busy schedule?

A: Trust me, I've been there. When we first started this natural healing journey, time felt super tight. But here's the thing—this journey is not about adding more to your plate; it's about simplifying. Look for time-wasters in your day. Trade 30 minutes of TV for a family walk outside. Prep whole foods in bulk on weekends. We started having "unplugged" evenings, turning off all devices and just hanging out together. It cut down on EMF (electromagnetic field) exposure and brought our family closer. Recent studies have suggested that exposure to various levels of EMFs are connected to toxic health effects, such as endocrine disruption and mental health disturbances ("EMFs: Health Impacts and Reducing Exposures," The Institute of Functional Medicine, 2024). Remember, every little change adds up. Natural healing happens in those small, everyday choices we make.

Q: How do I deal with skepticism from friends and family about our lifestyle changes?

A: Yeah, this is a tough one. When we moved to a farm, people thought we'd lost it. Here's what worked for us: First, just do your thing! As people see good changes in how you look and feel, they get curious. Share your story without preaching. It took years before our extended family started to catch on and began making their own changes. So be patient. Offer to cook a tasty plant-forward meal for your doubting friends. You're shaking up some deeply held generational beliefs about health and medicine. When you get criticism, be kind and stick to the facts—or better yet, maybe don't even respond to their apprehension. Just say, "I get it, it was hard for us at first as well." Talk about the research that got you started. Most importantly, stay true to your path. Your commitment to natural healing will speak louder than any argument.

Q: What if I'm not seeing immediate results from natural healing methods?

A: I totally get this worry. When we first cleaned up our diet and environment, I was hoping for overnight miracles. But natural healing isn't always quick. It's more like growing a garden than popping a pill. You're setting up the right conditions for health, and that takes time.

To help maintain momentum and stay positive, try keeping a journal to track small changes and victories. You might notice better sleep or mood before any physical improvements. Patience is key here. Trust and have faith in the process. Your body can do amazing things when given the right tools. Stick with it, and you'll likely start seeing good changes you didn't even expect.

Q: How can I make sure I'm getting all necessary nutrients on my new diet?

A: As previously mentioned, most Americans are deficient in at least one of the B vitamins, are low in magnesium and are deficient in potassium. These crucial nutrients are stripped from our food supply thanks to heavy processing, chemical spraying and genetic modification...the list goes on. It's no wonder so many of us are running on empty. The good news? Focusing on eating real, unprocessed and unadulterated foods can begin to correct these deficiencies—naturally.

This is a big one for anyone starting out with natural healing through food. When we first changed our diets, I was obsessed with maximizing nutrition with everything we ate. Here's what I learned.

Focus on variety. Eat lots of different fruits and veggies. Load up on leafy greens, beans, nuts and seeds—these give you tons of nutrients. Pay extra attention to vitamin B12, iron and omega-3s. We use nutritional yeast for B12, cook in cast iron pans for iron and add ground flaxseeds to smoothies for omega-3s. We also found local sources of grass-fed and finished beef and pastured poultry.

And because hidden deficiencies are so common, it's smart to think about getting your blood checked regularly to see if you're missing anything. A well-planned diet really can give you all you need and help your body heal naturally—especially when you're replenishing what modern food systems have taken away.

If you're serious about making this lifestyle work for you, our resources give you access to a curated list that can help you take your health to the next level (scan the QR code at the end of each chapter). It's one thing to follow general nutritional advice—it's another to have a roadmap tailored to you. Join us and take the guesswork out of your natural healing journey. We've created a resource to help you find real food sources anywhere in the US. We can even develop individualized protocols for individualized results with advanced biomarkers through our Connected Health platform.

Q: What if I'm experiencing detox symptoms as I transition to a more natural lifestyle?

A: Detox symptoms? Actually, that's a good sign. It means your body's getting rid of stored toxins. When we first cleaned up our diet and environment, I got headaches and felt wiped out. It was rough at first, but I learned to see it as a sign of healing. Here are some tips:

- Stay hydrated. It helps flush out toxins.
- Get plenty of rest. Your body's working overtime.
- Dry brushing and Epsom salt baths can help speed things up.
- Activated charcoal and buffered vitamin C are also great tools to support your body during detox—charcoal helps

adsorb toxins, while buffered vitamin C can aid in reducing inflammation and boosting your body's natural cleansing processes.

If your detox symptoms are bad or last too long, talk to a doctor who gets natural healing. Remember, this won't last forever. On the other side of detox is great health. Trust your body's wisdom and your ability to listen to it. It knows how to heal itself when given the right support.

For access to my detox protocol, check out our resource page accessible with the QR code in the book.

Q: *How do I balance natural healing approaches with necessary conventional medical care?*

A: This is tricky and often overlooked. Healing and total health are not about saying no to all traditional medicine. It's about finding a balance. When Anna was first diagnosed, we followed regular treatments. But we also looked into other options. We learned to be informed advocates. Question everything. Get second opinions. Do your homework. For us, using functional medicine ideas was key. We found a doctor who respected our choices and worked with us. Remember, you know your body best. Trust your gut. If something doesn't feel right, speak up. Natural healing can often work hand in hand with regular care, making a more complete approach to health. Our resource, *How to Talk to Your Doctor*, can help guide you through this process.

Q: *What if I'm feeling overwhelmed by all the information about toxins and environmental health?*

A: Been there. Even with my medical training and thirst for knowledge, when I first started researching crystal meth and how it affects the brain, I fell into a deep rabbit hole of info about toxins. It can be scary stuff. Here's what helped me:

- Focus on what you can control. Start with your home. Switch out chemical cleaners for natural ones.
- Choose organic food when you can.
- Filter your water.

Make these changes slowly. Remember, cutting down on toxins is a journey, not a race. Every small change counts. As you learn, share with others. Teaching helps you remember what you've learned. Most importantly, don't let fear of toxins steal your joy. Balance being aware with enjoying life. Natural healing is about thriving, not just surviving. We have an awesome resource for this based on a guide from the Harvard School of Public Health, accessible through the QR code below.

Believe it or not, feeling overwhelmed is a good sign. It means you're taking charge of your health. But it can be a lot. Give yourself breaks. Ask family or friends for help if you can. This is a marathon, not a sprint, so pace yourself. Celebrate every small win. With each bit of knowledge you gain, and each time you stand up for yourself, you're making progress. You're becoming your own best health advocate.

Q: How can I incorporate natural healing practices into my children's lives?

A: Getting kids into natural healing can be fun and rewarding. Make it an adventure. When we moved to the farm, our kids loved growing food. They learned about nutrition by taking care of plants. For little ones, start simple. Teach them about "eating the rainbow" to get different nutrients. Make natural remedies together—like honey and lemon for sore throats. Encourage playing outside. It's not just fun, it's great for their immune system and overall health. Be a good example. Kids learn more from what we do than what we say. When they see you putting natural health first, they'll follow your lead. Remember, teaching kids about natural healing sets them up for a lifetime of good health.

Q: What if I'm struggling to afford organic food and natural products on our budget?

A: This is a real worry for many families trying natural healing. Remember, perfect is the enemy of good. Do what you can with what you have. Choose what's most important. Use the Environmental Working Group's "Dirty Dozen" and "Clean Fifteen" lists to decide which produce to buy organic. Think about joining a Community Supported Agriculture (CSA) program or starting a small garden. Even a few pots on a windowsill can give you fresh herbs.

For natural household products, learn to make your own. We started making our cleaning products with vinegar and essential oils —it's cheaper and healthier. You can find online how to make these pretty simply. Remember, stress about money can undo the good of organic food. Find a balance that works for your family. Every step toward natural living, no matter how small, is a win for your health.

On a personal note, we couldn't afford it either as kids growing up. My dad grew up in the hills of West Virginia and planted fruit trees and a garden. We grew a good portion of our fruits and vegetables on our three-quarter-acre plot of land in Harrisonburg, Virginia. In hindsight, I can see that I got the bug to grow my own food when I was super young. But it started for me as a matter of necessity.

Want to take your natural healing journey even deeper? This isn't just what I do personally—it's my personal mission. I'm passionate about providing free, life-changing education to help you reclaim your health.

That's why I've created a space packed with invaluable resources —hundreds of in-depth blogs covering everything from detox, hormones and gut health to mold illness, Lyme disease and more. If you love to read, I've curated a vetted list of over 70 must-read books, each carefully selected from the 400+ I've personally devoured.

Prefer to learn while on the go? Tune into our YouTube channel and podcast (also found by following the QR code below), where we bring expert insights and practical solutions straight to you—wherever you are in your healing process.

This isn't just about information; it's about empowerment. I believe that true health starts with knowledge, and I'm committed to making sure you have access to the tools you need. Understanding your body is key because it allows you to take control of your health and transform your life. Start your journey today. Visit our website and discover the resources we've made available to you on our resource page (**AaronHartmanMD.com**). All these are waiting for you.

But I think it's important for you to understand the system you're fighting. From my unique position as a medical doctor and an advocate for a child with special medical needs, I am able to see how the system is failing patients from the inside out. In the next chapter, I am going to reveal a lot of secrets about medicine that no other doctor will tell you.

Scan the QR code below with your phone's camera. This will direct you to open a web page that provides instant access to our comprehensive collection of free resources.

6

___

THE HIDDEN TRUTH ABOUT HEALTHCARE

What I'm about to share isn't just surprising—it's transformative for how you'll view healthcare from this moment forward.

So let's start with the easy stuff. Do you know what the number one cause of death in our country currently is? It's heart disease. Each year, just shy of 700000 Americans die from cardiovascular conditions ("Leading Causes of Death (for US)," Center for Disease Control, 2025). Now, what do you think the second most common cause of death is? It's gaining ground so rapidly that within the next several years, based on current trends, it will become the new leader. What is it? Cancer. According to the Centers for Disease Control, roughly 600000 people die from cancer every year in the United States—a staggering number that continues to climb despite our technological advances and billions invested in research ("Leading Causes of Death (for US)," Center for Disease Control, 2025).

All right, so what's the number three cause of death in our country every year? Take a moment to think about it before I reveal the answer. Could it be dementia? Infectious diseases? Autoimmune disorders? It's none of these. In fact, none of them even come close. The number three cause of death in the United States is medical error. Over 250000 people each year succumb to mistakes made within our healthcare system ("Medical Error: The Third Leading Cause of Death in the US," Makary, 2016). Let that sink in for a moment—more Americans die annually from errors in their medical care than from stroke, respiratory disease, accidents, Alzheimer's or diabetes. A healthcare system designed to heal is, with alarming frequency, doing the opposite.

Is this really a new concept? Not at all. When I took the Hippocratic Oath upon entering medical school in 1996, I solemnly swore "to do no harm, to enter no home for evil, but only for good." These principles have been guiding physicians for over 2000 years—a testament to healthcare's long-recognized potential for harm. When I completed my residency back in 2003 to 2004, we already knew medical error was a serious issue. We studied it through the "Swiss cheese model" of system failure—how small mistakes, like holes in slices of cheese, could accidentally line up and lead to a tragedy (more on this later). Back then, we said iatrogenesis—the harm caused directly by medical treatment—was the fifth leading cause of death. This is just one aspect of medical error.

But a lot has changed since then. And not for the better.

You'd think that with newer technologies, stricter regulations like HIPAA and mandatory screenings for everything from vaccines to depression, the system would be safer. But it's not. In fact, one could argue all of these have just made it worse—slowing down care, burdening providers and shifting focus away from patients and toward bureaucratic compliance.

If we widen the lens to the entire US healthcare system, medical error may actually be the second leading cause of death. Possibly even the first. But the truth is...we don't really know because no one is tracking it! Not the way we track airline crashes or train derailments. The Federal Aviation Administration has a strict protocol: Every crash, every near miss, is investigated thoroughly. Systems are changed to prevent it from happening again. But in medicine? We do the opposite.

Doctors are terrified of being sued. There's an entire industry built around malpractice litigation. So when a mistake happens, it gets buried—never spoken of, never studied, never fixed. There's no safety net to protect healthcare providers from honest mistakes. Therefore, there's no incentive to be transparent. Reporting errors only brings on legal risk. No system like aviation's voluntary reporting. No culture of learning from near misses. Just silence...and more victims.

And that's why I'm sharing this jarring information (and insider secret) with you—because the system itself, the very one we're supposed to trust with our lives, is broken. And if medical error is the third leading cause of death, you have to ask yourself: Who's protecting you from it? The truth is, it's not your medical provider... it's not your hospital. It has to be you. You are your first line of defense.

When I left the military in 2007 and joined an established practice in Virginia, the founder warned me sternly: "You've got to watch out for your patients in the hospital. The specialists will kill them. The hospital will kill them. It's your job as their primary doctor to get them out alive." Back then, I thought he was being melodramatic and unnecessarily cynical. But in hindsight, he had intuitively recognized a harsh truth—if he wasn't vigilantly advocating for his patients, they might not make it out of the hospital alive. His words weren't hyperbole; they were a vital warning from a physician who had witnessed the third leading cause of death firsthand.

So what does medical error encompass, and why am I mentioning it?

Medical error encompasses a host of problems: misdiagnosis or delayed diagnosis, medication side effects and surgical complications, hospital-acquired infections and secondary complications like blood clots and pulmonary emboli that occur simply because patients are immobile for days or weeks at a time. It includes it all.

What's more disturbing is that the 250000 figure is likely a significant underestimate. Dr. Martin Makary's review of the Harvard data pointed out that these statistics were based solely on Medicare information from the elderly population—it didn't include teens, children or middle-aged adults. The true toll could be much higher, potentially making medical error the second or even number one leading cause of death in America. We may never know the full extent because, remarkably, the CDC does not officially track these deaths. When Dr. Makary tried to publish his findings, both the *New England Journal of Medicine* and the *Journal of the American Medical Association* refused to publish them, claiming this wasn't a problem of concern. He eventually had to publish in European medical literature (*Blind Spots: When Medicine Gets It Wrong, and What It Means for Our Health*, Makary, 2024). This institutional denial is not just ridiculous—it's dangerous. While I'm not here to dwell on this systemic failure, it is a critical context for understanding why you must approach healthcare differently.

My basic point is this: When I see a patient, the first thing I do is nothing. Counterintuitive as it sounds, doing something could actually harm or even kill the person. I pause, breathe and think. Then I carefully examine the current standard of care and ask whether there are alternatives at least as safe as what's conventionally practiced in our country. If these alternatives exist, I explore that pathway. If not, I'll adhere to established protocols. This deliberate approach—this conscious restraint—is exactly what we did with Anna. It's precisely what I do with every patient in my clinic. And this principle alone— simply not rushing to medicalize, not jumping to invasive procedures, not immediately reaching for the prescription pad—can dramatically improve patient outcomes by avoiding medication complications, surgical risks and the cascade of interventions that often follows the first medical touch. Sometimes the most powerful medical decision is the choice to wait, observe and truly understand before acting.

One of the first times I came face-to-face with this reality was while working in a mission hospital in Ecuador. A young boy arrived with meningitis—his mother had delayed bringing him to the hospital because in their culture, hospitals were places where people went to die. Her hesitation had allowed his pneumonia to progress to meningitis. When we inevitably had to admit him, she collapsed in grief. Her wails echoed down the hallway, a primal sound of maternal anguish. For her, hospitalization wasn't treatment—it was a death sentence. Her worst fears were materializing before her eyes. The good news, however, was that seven days later, her son walked out of the hospital, hand-in-hand with his relieved mother. That image has stayed with me for decades. In that culture, the fear of hospitals as death houses was so ingrained that this mother believed admission meant the end of her child's life.

In stark contrast, I believe we in America have lost a healthy skepticism of medicalization and institutionalization. The invasive procedures, the pharmaceutical interventions, the technological monitoring—all these have been sanitized and normalized under the veneer of progress, technology and science. We've forgotten that every medical touch carries risk, that hospitals themselves can be dangerous places and that sometimes the cure is indeed worse than the disease.

This returns us to the concept of blind spots—the critical areas of healthcare that we systematically overlook or ignore. Does our healthcare system demonstrate a healthy respect for its own limitations and potential for harm? Currently, the answer is a resounding no. I won't delve into the pandemic response here—that's a complex topic deserving its own book—but I'll invite you to reflect on how the principle of "first, do no harm" did or did not guide our national approach. It's not difficult to argue that, in our rush to act, we may have inflicted more collective harm than good. The lockdowns, the delayed medical care for non-COVID conditions, the mental health consequences and the educational disruptions—these represent potential blind spots of massive proportion. But my purpose isn't to dissect that particular crisis. Rather, it's to highlight how easily even well-intentioned medical systems can lose sight of their primary obligation to avoid harm while pursuing healing.

This is precisely where integrative and functional medicine—whatever label you prefer—becomes vital. These approaches offer evidence-based alternatives that not only match the safety profile of conventional care but often produce superior outcomes. The difference? They require genuine patient engagement, personal ownership of your health journey and a true partnership with a skilled practitioner who can navigate these waters alongside you. The ultimate goal for anyone reading this book should be to become actively involved in their healthcare decisions—to transform from passive recipient to informed participant. Educate yourself about your specific conditions. Understand the broader context of health and our healthcare system. Develop the confidence to ask questions and the wisdom to recognize when to seek alternatives. This shift in mindset alone could help you avoid becoming one of the 250000 annual victims of the third most common cause of death in our country. If this is the only lesson you take from these pages, this book will have been priceless for you—because this knowledge might literally save your life.

I've vetted several powerful books on this topic that you'll find on our website's reading list (visit **AaronHartmanMD.com** or scan the QR code at the end of this chapter for all of my free resources). From *The Immortal Life of Henrietta Lacks* by Rebecca Skloot to *Blind Spots* and *The Price We Pay* by Dr. Marty Makary, *Missing Microbes* by Martin J. Blaser and *The Disease Delusion* by Jeffrey Bland—each offers crucial insights into our healthcare system's hidden dangers. These five books alone will transform your perspective on modern medicine.

In today's world, where we have unprecedented technology and access to information, being an uninformed patient is no longer an option—it's potentially deadly. You must become both an educated consumer and an active participant in your healthcare decisions. The stakes are simply too high to delegate this responsibility entirely to anyone else, no matter their credentials or intentions.

I hope this little journey off the beaten path was useful for you. It's something I think about daily in my practice. I talk about it routinely with patients. If nothing else, staying as healthy as possible to stay out of the healthcare system for as long as possible will pay tremendous dividends with your health and longevity. This isn't just advice—it's a survival strategy in a system where good intentions don't always lead to good outcomes. That's why this entire chapter—

and really this entire book—is about patient empowerment. Because even though we didn't realize it at the time, what we were doing with Anna—questioning protocols, seeking alternatives, building our own care team—wasn't just about getting better outcomes: We were protecting our daughter from the system itself.

And now, more than ever, that's exactly what you need to do. If you remember anything from Anna's story, remember this: Being your own advocate is not a luxury—it's a matter of survival.

So as you continue your journey with us, keep this in mind. The healthcare system is not neutral. It's not always safe. And you must be equipped to navigate it, question it and sometimes even push against it. Because your life—or the life of someone you love—may depend on it.

The Swiss Cheese Model

Imagine several slices of Swiss cheese stacked on top of each other. Each slice represents a different safety layer in the healthcare system—protocols, double-checks, supervision and technology. The holes in each slice represent potential failures. This is how I was taught that medical errors occurred in our healthcare system.

Most of the time, the holes don't line up, so problems are caught before they cause harm. But occasionally, the holes align perfectly, creating a clear path from error to catastrophe. A tired resident misreads a decimal point. A pharmacist doesn't catch the mistake. A nurse administers the wrong dose. A patient dies.

But here's what medical school didn't teach me: This model only addresses obvious, dramatic failures—surgical errors, medication mistakes, procedural complications. It completely ignores the far more common ways that medicine itself harms patients.

What about the patient prescribed antidepressants who develops sexual dysfunction and weight gain that destroys their marriage? The chronic pain patient who becomes dependent on opioids prescribed by their trusted physician? These are iatrogenesis—harm caused by medical treatment. What about the elderly patient who catches pneumonia during a hospital stay and never fully recovers? Medical harm. Another form of medical injury that the Swiss cheese model never addresses.

The tragic irony? These aren't system failures or aligned holes—they're often the direct result of simply engaging with the healthcare system. The system works exactly as designed, yet still causes harm.

I learned this broader reality only after years in practice, when patients began arriving at my office not just with their original conditions, but with additional problems created by the very treatments they'd received. The person with high cholesterol started on a statin drug then over years develops diabetes and peripheral neuropathy from that drug. Or the person with hypertension started on a fluid pill, a diuretic, who develops low-level magnesium and potassium deficiencies from the medicine. Over years this can lead to palpitations and another drug, a beta blocker. This combination increases insulin resistance and over time can lead to diabetes (*Iatrogenicity: Causes and Consequences of Iatrogenesis in Cardiovascular Medicine*, Gussak et al., 2017). I was witnessing iatrogenesis on a massive scale—systematic harm that goes far beyond the narrow definition of "medical error" they taught us in school.

A History of Dangerous Certainty

As we talked about in Chapter Three, medicine has blind spots, and they're more common than you might think. These glaring gaps in our understanding are firmly established "truths" about patient care that are later proven false, wrong or woefully incomplete. These aren't simple mistakes but fundamental misunderstandings that can persist for decades, affecting countless lives. Addressing these blind spots often requires a complete paradigm shift—a total reimagining of how we understand health and disease. Sometimes this change comes gradually through accumulated evidence; other times, it takes just one determined researcher willing to stand alone against prevailing wisdom, risking ridicule and professional isolation to break through entrenched thinking and forge a new path forward.

This is how medicine truly advances—not through consensus, but through courage.

Take stomach ulcers. For years, doctors swore they were caused by stress and spicy foods. It took two maverick doctors, Barry Marshall and Robin Warren, to prove that most ulcers were actually caused by a bacterium called H. pylori. They had to fight the medical establishment for years before their discovery was accepted ("Ulcers, Stress and the Discovery of Helicobacter pylori," Crenner, 2024).

Dr. Marshall's story is unusually unique in that he infected himself with the bacteria, got stomach ulcers, was scoped to prove he had ulcers, took antibiotics and then got rescoped to show the ulcers had healed. It took years to get this published, but eventually he won the Nobel Prize for this work. That is crazy commitment and courage!

Healthcare's blind spots aren't new—they're woven into the fabric of medical history. Understanding this pattern isn't about dwelling on past mistakes; it's about recognizing that today's "established truths" may be tomorrow's embarrassments.

Semmelweis Injustice

In 1847, Hungarian physician Ignaz Semmelweis made a shocking discovery. He noticed that women giving birth in the ward run by doctors and medical students died at rates three times higher than those in the ward run by midwives. The cause? Childbed fever, a mysterious illness that was killing new mothers within days of delivery.

Semmelweis observed that doctors often came directly from performing autopsies to delivering babies—without washing their hands. When he instituted mandatory handwashing with chlorinated lime solution, the death rate plummeted from 18 percent to less than two percent.

The medical establishment's response? They ridiculed and ostracized him. Senior physicians were offended by the suggestion that their hands could be unclean. The idea that gentlemen's hands could harbor disease was considered preposterous.

Eventually Semmelweis was dismissed from his position, suffered a nervous breakdown, was put in jail for this heresy and died in an asylum—ironically, from an infection that proper handwashing might have prevented ("Hand Hygiene: Semmelweis' Lesson Through Céline's Pen," Braut and Zatta, 2023.). It took decades before handwashing became standard practice in hospitals.

The lesson isn't just about handwashing—it's about how medical orthodoxy can reject life saving discoveries when they challenge established beliefs.

The Tobacco Tragedy

For over half a century, the medical establishment got smoking spectacularly wrong. Despite mounting evidence, it took 7000 research studies and over 50 years of preventable deaths before the Surgeon General finally declared that smoking causes lung cancer.

What's particularly sobering is how the medical profession was complicit in this delay. Cigarette advertisements featured endorsements from physicians. Medical journals accepted tobacco advertising revenue. The very people trusted to protect public health became unwitting accomplices in one of the greatest health catastrophes in human history.

The Hormone Catastrophe

More recently, we've witnessed the whiplash of hormone replacement therapy recommendations. For decades, hormone therapy was thought to be protective against heart disease and osteoporosis. Then, seemingly overnight, with the Women's Health Initiative in 2002 it became dangerous—associated with increased cancer and cardiovascular risks.

Now, in 2025, we're witnessing another reversal. Bioidentical hormone therapy is being recognized as beneficial when properly administered, and we're realizing that the previous studies had serious methodological flaws. Women who suffered through years of menopausal symptoms because they were told hormones were dangerous are now discovering they were denied helpful treatment based on flawed research. These aren't just academic footnotes—they represent millions of lives affected by medical blind spots.

Why Smart Doctors Miss Obvious Solutions

Understanding the limitations of the medical system and why doctors practice the way they do can help you navigate your health-care more effectively and find the right physician or provider to help you heal.

The Silo Effect: Specialists Who Can't See the Forest

Modern medical education trains doctors to become increasingly specialized, creating experts who know more and more about less and less. This creates a dangerous fragmentation of care—here are some examples:

Cardiologists see only the heart—they might miss how gut inflammation affects cardiovascular health.

Gastroenterologists focus only on endoscopy procedures—they often overlook how the gut microbiome, stress and trauma manifest as gut symptoms and systemic health.

Psychiatrists treat only the mind—they may ignore nutritional deficiencies that cause depression and anxiety.

Endocrinologists manage only hormones—they frequently miss environmental toxins that disrupt endocrine function.

The result? Patients ping-pong between specialists, each treating isolated symptoms without anyone examining the interconnected whole. I regularly see patients who've been to five or six specialists without anyone asking the most basic question: "What's causing all of these seemingly unrelated problems?"

Anna's story perfectly illustrates this fragmentation. At age four, we consulted three different specialists about her muscle tone:

The **physiatrist** recommended Botox injections and specialized casting.

The **orthopedic surgeon** pushed for heel cord lengthening surgery.

The **physical therapist** suggested a surgically implanted baclofen pump.

Three experts, three completely different—and invasive—recommendations for the same child. None suggested the simple, non-invasive electrical stimulation device that ultimately proved more effective than any of their proposed procedures.

How is this possible? Each specialist was operating within their narrow domain of expertise, unable or unwilling to consider solutions outside their training. No one was able to fill in the gaps between the specialists. I had to become the specialist of the gray zones or the space between specialists—luckily, I was a medical doctor, an advantage that most parents don't have. Over time I learned that the gaps I was filling are what integrative and functional medicine are.

The Liability Trap: When Fear Drives Decisions

From the first day of medical school, physicians are warned: "Every patient is a potential lawsuit." This creates a defensive mindset that prioritizes legal protection over optimal care.

During my training, I heard variations of these warnings repeatedly:

You can't give a patient prolonged antibiotics for a tick-borne illness; it's potential malpractice.

You can't take away a patient's psych meds without a significant legal risk.

Any deviation from the standard of care risks a lawsuit.

This fear-based approach leads to several dangerous patterns:

Over-testing and over-treatment: Providers order excessive tests and procedures not because they're medically necessary, but because they provide legal cover. The mindset becomes "better safe than sorry," even when the interventions carry significant risks.

Resistance to innovation: New approaches, even when supported by research, are avoided because they fall outside established "standard of care" guidelines. This creates a system that's inherently conservative and slow to adopt beneficial changes.

Protocol-driven care: Providers follow algorithmic decision trees created by "evidence-based medicine" guidelines for generalized patient care rather than thinking critically about individual cases. While protocols can be helpful, especially early on in one's training, they often miss the nuances that make each patient unique and that a practitioner learns as they become more seasoned.

The Evidence-Based Medicine Illusion

Modern medicine prides itself on being "evidence-based," but there's a dirty secret: Much of that evidence is fundamentally flawed.

Dr. John Ioannidis's groundbreaking 2005 essay, "Why Most Published Research Findings Are False," revealed a shocking truth: Due to small sample sizes, researcher bias, selective reporting and financial conflicts of interest, **over 50 percent of published medical**

research cannot be reproduced ("Why Most Published Research Findings Are False," Ioannidis, 2005).

Think about that for a moment. Half of the "scientific evidence" driving medical decisions is unreliable. Yet doctors are trained to follow this evidence without question, and patients are expected to trust it completely.

Originally, evidence-based medicine was supposed to rest on three pillars:

1. Current research
2. Clinical experience
3. Patient preference

Today's system has eliminated patient preference as "unscientific" and dismissed clinical experience as "anecdotal," leaving only what many times is corporate-funded research—much of which is unreliable—to guide medical decisions.

This creates a system where physicians become technicians following flawed protocols rather than healers using their judgment, experience and understanding of individual patients.

Physician or Specialist Red Flags: System-Wide Warning Signs

After decades of practice and thousands of patient interactions, I've learned to recognize warning signs that suggest a practitioner is not aware of these systematic problems in healthcare delivery. They haven't seasoned their training with years of patient care experience. Being able to recognize these signs has helped me navigate care for my family, and it can help you, too.

You may not be a medical doctor, but you can also learn to recognize these red flags and adjust your care plan accordingly—they can help you identify when you might need to seek a second opinion or different approach:

Communication Red Flags

"It's all in your head"—When physicians can't find an obvious cause for your symptoms, they may default to psychological explanations rather than investigating further. This is particularly common with complex conditions like chronic fatigue, fibromyalgia or autoimmune diseases.

"Your labs are normal"—The assertion here is that nothing serious is wrong with you. Standard lab ranges are based on statistical averages, not optimal health. A physician who dismisses your symptoms because labs fall within "normal" ranges may be missing functional medicine insights about optimal versus acceptable levels.

"There's nothing more we can do"—This phrase often means "There's nothing more I know how to do," rather than "Nothing can be done." It may be time to seek care from practitioners with different training or approaches.

Dismissing your research—While you shouldn't expect doctors to follow internet theories, a well-trained and experienced physician will know their limits and be open to other options. One who becomes defensive or dismissive when you bring legitimate questions or research may not be the right partner for your health journey.

Treatment Red Flags

Immediate jump to prescription drugs—Without exploring lifestyle factors, environmental triggers or root causes, most practitioners will reflexively reach for pharmaceutical solutions to complex problems.

Resistance to discussing alternatives—A healthcare provider who won't even discuss complementary approaches or lifestyle interventions may have a narrow perspective on healing.

No discussion of prevention—Practitioners focused only on treating existing problems without addressing prevention may be missing opportunities for more comprehensive care.

Hurried appointments—Consistent 10 to 15-minute visits for complex chronic conditions suggest a system prioritizing volume over quality of care.

Care Coordination Red Flags

Frequent medication changes without explanation—If your medications are constantly being adjusted without clear reasoning or improvement in symptoms, the underlying approach may be flawed.

Multiple specialists with no coordination—When you're seeing several specialists who don't communicate with each other, you risk fragmented care and dangerous interactions.

Emergency room visits for chronic conditions—If you repeatedly end up in emergency care for ongoing health issues, your chronic care isn't adequately addressing root causes.

Feeling worse after following medical advice—Sometimes treatments make things worse before they get better, but consistent decline following medical recommendations warrants serious re-evaluation.

The Economics of Error: Following the Money

UNDERSTANDING the financial incentives in healthcare can help explain why certain problems persist and why change is often slow. Here are some perverse incentives many patients encounter as they try to navigate the system:

Volume over value: The current system rewards doctors for seeing more patients and performing more procedures, not for achieving better outcomes. A physician who spends an hour with a complex case earns less than one who sees three patients over the same time ("The Triple Aim: Care, Health, And Cost," Berwick et al., 2008).

Defensive medicine: Fear of lawsuits drives expensive, unnecessary testing and procedures. Studies suggest that 20 to 30 percent of medical interventions are primarily defensive rather than therapeutic ("The Cost of Defensive Medicine on Three Hospital Medicine Services," Rothberg et al., 2014).

Pharmaceutical influence: While direct payments to physicians have become more transparent, pharmaceutical companies still spend billions influencing medical education, research and practice patterns ("Industry-Funded Medical Education is Always Promotion," Adriane Fugh-Berman, 2021).

Specialist referrals: The system financially rewards referrals to specialists over comprehensive primary care, leading to fragmented, expensive care ("Trends in Physician Referrals in the United States, 1999-2009," Barnett et al., 2012).

The True Cost of Medical Errors

Medical errors don't just cost lives—they cost money. Healthcare-associated infections alone cost the US healthcare system over $17 billion annually. Medication errors cost an additional $21 billion per year ("The $17.1 Billion Problem: The Annual Cost Of Measurable Medical Errors," Van Den Bos et al., 2011). These aren't just statistics —they represent preventable suffering and waste.

Yet the system has little incentive to transparently report and learn from these errors. Hospitals and healthcare systems often view error reporting as a liability risk rather than an improvement opportunity.

Understanding these systematic problems isn't meant to create fear or distrust—it's meant to empower you to navigate the healthcare system more effectively. Here's how to protect yourself and your family:

A Personal Reflection

When I took the Hippocratic Oath in 1996, I solemnly swore "to do no harm." Those words have echoed in my mind throughout my career, especially as I've witnessed the unintended consequences of well-intentioned medical care.

The healthcare system's problems aren't primarily caused by bad people—they're caused by bad systems. Most healthcare providers entered their professions to help people heal. But they're working within structures that often prioritize efficiency over effectiveness, volume over value and conformity over innovation.

The most sobering realization of my career has been recognizing how often the system itself becomes an obstacle to healing. When I see patients who've been made worse by multiple interventions, who've been told their conditions are "uncurable" without proper investigation or who've been dismissed when they didn't respond to standard treatments, I'm witnessing the cost of systematic blind spots.

This isn't about rejecting modern medicine—it's about demanding better from our providers. It's about recognizing that the same system that can perform miraculous surgeries and cure devastating infections can also miss simple solutions to complex problems, and holding it accountable.

The Path Forward

Healthcare is at a crossroads. We can continue with the current system—accepting medical error as an inevitable cost of doing business—or we can demand fundamental changes that prioritize patient outcomes over institutional convenience.

The transformation begins with you. You are contributing to a shift toward more patient-centered, effective healthcare every time you:

- Ask thoughtful questions during medical visits.
- Seek second opinions for important decisions.
- Research your conditions and treatments.
- Advocate for comprehensive rather than fragmented care.
- Share your experiences with others.

The hidden truth about healthcare is uncomfortable but essential: *The system designed to heal you can also harm you.* Medical errors are not rare accidents—they're a predictable consequence of systematic problems that affect every aspect of healthcare delivery.

But here's the empowering truth: Once you understand these limitations, you can navigate around them. You can become an informed healthcare consumer, build a supportive care team and make decisions that truly serve your health rather than institutional convenience.

Your life is too precious to leave entirely in the hands of any system, no matter how well-intentioned your providers are. By understanding healthcare's hidden truths and taking an active role in your care, you're not just protecting yourself—you're modeling a new way of engaging with medicine that could benefit everyone. I know firsthand how navigating the medical maze is daunting and intimidating —so I'm here to give you some tips and some success stories. I hope I've solved some of modern medicine's mysteries for you, but keep reading to learn more about how to advocate for yourself.

The stakes couldn't be higher. Knowledge of these systematic problems could literally save your life. Use it wisely.

Scan the QR code below with your phone's camera. This will direct you to open a web page that provides instant access to our comprehensive collection of free resources.

7

MODERN MEDICINE'S MEDICAL MAZE

Anna and her cerebral palsy diagnosis changed our world forever. We went to the best specialist we could find, hoping for clear answers, but instead, we found ourselves trapped in a maze of conflicting opinions and endless recommendations for surgeries. It felt like the system was more focused on fixing symptoms than helping Anna actually grow and thrive.

The healthcare system isn't built for kids like Anna, or really anyone with a complex medical condition. It's a machine designed to churn out the same generic solutions for everyone known as the standard of care. For us, it felt like trying to jam a square peg into a round hole. Every step was a fight—nothing came easy.

Take Anna's need for glasses. She had strabismus, an eye condition where her eyes wobbled uncontrollably. The standard glasses were these hard, ugly things that constantly fell off and were completely useless. But my wife, Becky—ever the researcher—knew that vision was critical for hand-eye coordination and brain development. She refused to settle.

We were living in Tampa at the time, and Becky searched the entire state for a specific type of glasses that would actually help Anna. She discovered a brand called Miraflex, but no one carried them or even knew about them. Luckily, she eventually found an eye doctor willing to work with us and special-order them just for Anna. It was exhausting and frustrating—but she did it. Now, 15 years later, those types of glasses are everywhere, easily available. But back then? It was one of many battles.

Everything for Anna was like that—a fight, a struggle. At first, everything seemed impossible, but we pushed through, with faith as our constant companion. That's the reality of special-needs medicine. The system isn't built for individual needs and nuanced care, so it's especially not built for kids like Anna. It's built for efficiency, for standard solutions and for quick fixes that check boxes rather than transform lives. It's a one-size-fits-all machine, more interested in throughput than outcomes, more aligned with the priorities of the medical industrial complex than with the needs of actual humans. So families like ours are left to fend for ourselves—to dig, to research and to challenge the experts who insist they know best, even when the best they offer is a barely functional status quo.

We were never looking for miracles. We were looking for someone—anyone—who would see Anna as a whole person. Not a chart. Not a diagnosis. Not a problem to be managed. Because when a system isn't designed to see people, it fails them—and that risk of failure became my burden to carry.

Doctors only told us what Anna *couldn't* do. They were focused on limitations. But we refused to let a diagnosis define her future. We learned to say *no*—no to unnecessary surgeries, no to cookie-cutter treatments, no to a future dictated by disability.

One of the biggest battles we fought was over mobility. Specialists had decided that Anna would never walk. Every treatment option they offered was based on that assumption—procedures to minimize pain, surgeries to make her look "better" in a wheelchair, interventions to make her seem more "normal." But Anna was never going to look "normal"—and that wasn't the goal anyway. The goal was for her to be *her best*, whatever that looked like for *her*.

We butted heads with the specialists over and over. Every time we asked, "Would this procedure make Anna better off 10 years from now?" the answer was almost always "No" or "We don't know."

One specific example was a surgical procedure to lengthen the tendons and ligaments in her legs because they were tight. This is a pretty normal issue in kids with cerebral palsy or even adults with traumatic brain injuries. These tight heel cords can cause pain, prevent a person from standing straight up and can impact walking. This is just one of the many downstream effects of significant brain injuries—the muscles in the legs get tight and nonfunctional. But the surgery to address this would have permanently taken away any hope of Anna ever walking. Still, they pushed it—because it would make her legs look more "typical" and better in a wheel chair. That wasn't a good enough reason for us to agree to a life-altering surgery.

Instead, we traveled to Dupont Children's Hospital in Delaware to see the leading expert—the man who literally wrote the book on cerebral palsy. His team had a completely different approach. Yes, they had alternative procedures they could do—their recommendation was a medical device called a baclofen spinal pump that would be implanted in her back. But they recommended we wait—not necessarily because it was the best thing for Anna long-term, but because she was too small at the time to safely perform the procedure. Still, all I heard was, "You can wait." There's no rush. And in that moment, that was all we needed to hear.

So we waited. And just by *not* rushing into that one set of procedures, we changed the course of Anna's future.

In the meantime, I threw myself into researching alternative ways to improve muscle tone—everything from massage to electrical and magnetic stimulation. We explored every avenue. At that time there wasn't much research on kids with cerebral palsy and nothing on kids with brain injury from crystal meth exposure, so I had to dive into parallel literature on adults with traumatic brain injuries and neurological conditions like multiple sclerosis. Though not the exact same, they share similar mechanisms of action—plus, I had nothing else to go on. This is called translational medicine, when you take research from a similar but different situation and translate it to other similar but different conditions.

Now, more than 10 years later, she still hasn't had a single surgical procedure. And despite everything we were told—despite the certainty of the specialists—Anna *can* walk. With crutches, yes, but she can do it. If we had followed through with the first recommended, status-quo procedure, that would never have been.

You might think pushing back against doctors is risky—and yeah, it can be. But we found that saying *no* often led us to *better* options. Even saying "not now" is often a better option. While doctors were focused on just managing symptoms and keeping the status quo, we kept looking. We explored alternative therapies. We focused on nutrition. We found practitioners who treated Anna as a whole person, not just a list of medical conditions.

We used to have a Sprinter van, like the Amazon vans that come to your home, so that we could fit all of Anna's equipment into it. One day, I rolled her out to the van in her wheelchair, opened the door and went back inside the house to get some stuff. When I came back out, she had already gotten out of her chair, walked up into the van and put herself into it. I was amazed—happy beyond words—but at the same time, terrified that she could have fallen and hurt herself. Yet the ability to do this is nothing short of miraculous for the little girl who was never supposed to walk, talk or crawl. That single moment encapsulated what years of fighting, research and saying *no* to the status quo had led to.

Anna defied every gloomy prediction. At 19, she is able to get in and out of her wheelchair by herself, put her clothes on by herself and walk with her crutches (with a spotter standing by, just in case). Last year she was swimming with a life jacket, and could get in and out of the pool with assistance. But she is always surprising us—this spring she started swimming without a life jacket. She has a spotter standing by and is able to get herself out of the pool without help, but this kid was supposed to be a vegetable. She continues to thrive. A diagnosis is just a *starting point*—not the end of the road!

I'm not suggesting that you abandon traditional medicine. The key is to find doctors who *listen*, who *respect* your choices, who work *with* you instead of against you. You can't just let things happen *to you*; you have to be actively working toward things working *for you*.

I can already hear the criticisms. "Alternative medicine isn't proven!" Yet in places like Canada and Europe, they're already integrating alternative methods successfully. And the Cleveland Clinic is the largest functional medicine clinic in the US. These places are out there—you just have to know where to look and be willing to do the work. "Fighting the system is too hard!" And sure, it is. But the cost of not fighting? That's even higher.

If you're feeling lost after a diagnosis, know this: You have power. You can ask questions. You can demand better. The hardest path often leads to the greatest victories. Our journey continues—full of highs, lows, breakthroughs and setbacks—but one thing has never changed: our mission to unlock Anna's full potential. And by fighting for her, we've discovered we're also clearing the path for countless others.

What makes this journey so profound is how Anna's "full potential" keeps evolving. At age 10, she could recognize and read single words. By 15, she could write them herself. Today, she's texting her friends and loved ones—reading, understanding, responding—all on her own, with no help, no prompts. That's not just progress; that's transformation. And it's a reminder that potential isn't fixed—it grows when we fight for it.

The system won't change for us. So we go around it. Or we push straight through it. Because a family's love—armed with knowledge, relentless determination and unshakable faith that it's going to work itself out and be okay—is unstoppable.

Anna has taught us that the best medicine isn't always in a pill. It's in believing, in fighting, in never giving up. And that's what we keep doing—day after day.

Many people feel like we did at the beginning of our battle for Anna—stuck in a health rut with no way out. It's rough. But like Frodo's journey in *The Lord of the Rings*, there's always a path forward —even when the road seems dark and impossible. Anna's story proves that even in hopeless situations there can be a way out. This is your quest, your journey with the "Ring of Power." And just like any great adventure, you need a team to help you succeed: a trusted Samwise to walk beside you, a wise Gandalf to guide you and even an unexpected Sauron—the challenges that force you to grow stronger.

Anna's journey didn't just change her life—it changed mine as a doctor. What I learned through helping her shaped how I approach every patient. And because of that, I was able to help patients like Lizzy.

Lizzy was a 15-year-old girl battling an unseen enemy. Like every child of her age, the pandemic had shaken her. Returning to school left her uneasy and anxious. But what she was experiencing went far beyond stress. She felt constantly lightheaded, dizzy and nauseous—like she might collapse at any moment. Fogged thinking made it impossible to focus.

Yet every doctor dismissed her case. "It's just anxiety. It's all in your head," they told her. They handed her medications that only made her feel worse. With no answers and no hope, her mother brought her to me.

In just 30 minutes of listening to her story, I had a strong suspicion: POTS (postural orthostatic tachycardia syndrome). POTS is a condition where the body doesn't properly regulate blood pressure or heart rate when changing positions—such as standing up. This leads to symptoms like lightheadedness, dizziness and a rapid increase in heart rate. It's a condition I see all the time—one that's frequently overlooked. (Visit our resource page using the QR code at the end of this chapter to find out more about this disorder with our POTS patient resource guide.)

I performed a simple exam, a variation of the "tilt table test." Lizzy lay down while I checked her blood pressure and pulse. Then I had her sit up and I checked it again. Her heart rate went up 15 beats per minute. Then I had her stand up and lean against the wall.

I lost her pulse. Her symptoms exploded. Her upper blood pressure number dropped below 90. Her heart rate skyrocketed to 140

BPM. When I asked how she felt, she was dizzy and starting to get a panic attack, saying, "My anxiety is getting really bad."

But this wasn't anxiety at all—it was POTS. And no other doctor had seen it.

Once we had the correct diagnosis, everything changed. We implemented a comprehensive protocol: dietary modifications to stabilize blood sugar, increased fluid and electrolyte intake, compression stockings to improve circulation and targeted physical exercises to retrain her autonomic nervous system. I also prescribed low-dose naltrexone, which research shows can reduce the brain inflammation associated with POTS.

Within weeks, Lizzy's "anxiety" began to improve. Within months, she was back to her normal activities, attending school regularly and living the life of a typical teenager. The transformation was so dramatic that her previous doctors could hardly believe it was the same patient.

Lizzy's story illustrates a critical point: When we look deeper, beyond surface symptoms and easy labels, we often find treatable root causes that conventional medicine overlooks entirely.

Why So Many Patients Are Overlooked

This is where so many people's journeys falter. Like Frodo being told to simply "stay in the Shire," patients are told to ignore their symptoms, that it's all in their head. They're handed medications that don't work—or worse, make them sicker. And when those fail, they're often told either "It's all in your head," or "We can't help you."

But the truth is, they can be helped. Functional medicine doctors take a different approach. Instead of dismissing symptoms, we dig deeper. Patients like Lizzy get real diagnoses for conditions like:

- Chronic Lyme disease
- Mold-related illness
- POTS
- Dysautonomia

- Mast cell activation syndrome (MCAS)
- Autoimmune diseases
- Hypermobility or hEDS

These aren't rare conditions anymore. They are the new normal.

The New Normal

Look at these shocking numbers:

- Eighteen percent of kids under 12 take prescription medications ("Prescription Drug Use in the US, 2015-2016," Martin et al., 2019).
- Almost 30 percent of teens between the ages of 12 and 18 have taken some kind of medication.
- Two-thirds of American adults are on at least one prescription drug ("Percentage of Adults Aged 18 and Older Who Took Prescription Medication During the Past 12 Months," Cohen and Mykyta, 2023).

And yet chronic illness is rising. IQ levels are dropping. ADHD and autism are becoming more common. Even Alzheimer's is showing up earlier. In 2023, the youngest case of Alzheimer's dementia was reported—a 19-year-old patient in China ("The Mysterious Case of the Youngest Person Ever Diagnosed With Alzheimer's," Cassella, 2024). This is not supposed to be normal, and we should not accept it.

By now you have a pretty clear illustration of the mess we're in. So now what? What do we do with all this information? We have to challenge it. I know you're probably thinking "Easy for you to say. You're a doctor." Well, I'm going to teach you how to confidently stand up for yourself and to build an arsenal of tools that will help you do it. You don't have to be a doctor to know how to talk to doctors, how to question a diagnosis and how to recognize flaws in a diagnosis or treatment plan. You just have to be informed. That's what I'm here for.

SCAN THE QR code below with your phone's camera. This will direct you to open a web page that provides instant access to our comprehensive collection of free resources.

PART II

CHALLENGING THE
STATUS QUO

8

THE EMPOWERED PATIENT

Many people feel overwhelmed by the healthcare system —reduced to mere cogs in a vast, impersonal machine. The paperwork, the rushed appointments, the confusing medical jargon, the fragmented care—it can leave even the most determined patient feeling powerless and lost. We've all been there, sitting in sterile waiting rooms, clutching referral forms, wondering if anyone actually sees us as a person rather than just another case number. But here's the truth: You have far more power than the system wants you to believe. Let's discuss how you can reclaim control of your health journey. You can transform yourself from passive patient to an empowered self advocate and create a personalized system that is designed for efficiency—one that helps you heal.

The Stark Contrast in Medical Outcomes

Before we dive into strategies for patient empowerment, let's look at a real-world example of how the system often fails patients—and how questioning standard protocols can lead to dramatically different outcomes.

Take Anna's case. She was born with severe cerebral palsy, a condition that, under conventional medical care, often leads to multiple surgeries, heavy medication use and frequent hospitalizations. By the time most children with her condition reach age 19, they've had up to 13 surgeries and countless hospital stays. But Anna? She's had zero surgeries, no hospital stays and only one round of antibiotics since we have had her. How is this possible?

We refused to blindly follow the "standard of care"—that official protocol physicians hide behind when recommending interventions they've been taught are necessary. Instead, we scrutinized every recommendation, demanding evidence and exploring alternatives before consenting to any treatment. While specialists pushed increasingly invasive interventions—baclofen pumps implanted in the spine, dorsal rhizotomy that would permanently sever nerves and multiple orthopedic surgeries to reshape her developing body—we discovered something the medical establishment had overlooked: a simple $300 electrical stimulation device that accomplished what all those invasive procedures promised to do. Without surgery! No hospital stays, no anesthesia risks, no irreversible changes to her nervous system—just a straightforward tool that respected her body's capacity to heal on its own terms.

This contrast isn't just about one child; it's about a systemic failure in modern medicine. The healthcare system is designed like an assembly line, where practitioners apply a one-size-fits-all approach rather than treating patients as individuals. While this works for simple, acute conditions (like infections, broken bones, appendicitis and an acute heart attack), it falls apart when addressing complex, chronic health issues—which are now alarmingly common.

Recognizing Systemic Issues in Your Own Healthcare Experience

Think back to your last few doctor visits or hospital stays. Certain moments likely stand out in stark relief against the blur of medical forms and sterile rooms. Perhaps you felt rushed—the doctor's hand already on the doorknob while you frantically tried to explain that one symptom you hadn't mentioned yet. Maybe you noticed the physician typing frantically into a computer, making more eye contact with the screen than with you. Or perhaps you left one specialist's office with a treatment plan, only to have another specialist completely contradict it days later, leaving you caught in the middle, confused and increasingly desperate. These moments of disconnection aren't just uncomfortable—they're revealing cracks in a system that's forgotten its purpose.

These experiences are not isolated incidents or simply bad luck —they're predictable symptoms of a fundamentally broken health-care system. The assembly-line approach to medicine prioritizes volume over understanding, procedures over people and billing codes over healing. Anna's journey proves that medicine as currently practiced must be completely reimagined from the ground up. Her story demonstrates that blindly accepting medical advice can lead to unnecessary interventions that alter lives forever. Instead, patients must develop a new set of skills: the ability to criti-cally analyze their healthcare experiences, recognize patterns of systemic failure, question inconsistencies without apology and advo-cate persistently for care that makes sense. This isn't just about getting better treatment—it's about fundamentally changing the power dynamic between patient and provider. The stakes couldn't be higher; as Anna's case shows, the difference between standard protocols and thoughtful care can literally change the trajectory of a life.

The Flaws in Medical Thinking: Why Doctors Miss the Big Picture

A recurring theme throughout Anna's journey was the over-whelming stream of contradictory medical advice. At just four years old, we met with a physical medicine specialist who proposed Botox injections and specially designed casts to help with her muscle tone. But when we consulted an orthopedic surgeon shortly after, the recommendation took a sharp turn—they strongly pushed for heel tendon lengthening surgery. Later, at an academic orthopedic center, the suggestion changed yet again: implant a baclofen pump in her back to manage the same muscle tone.

Three visits. Three completely different—and invasive—treatment plans. How could multiple specialists, each evaluating the same child, arrive at such drastically different conclusions?

That glaring contradiction opened our eyes to a deeper truth about the medical system:

- Why were these experts offering such disparate opinions?
- Why did every path seem to leap straight to an extreme solution?
- Why wasn't anyone suggesting non-invasive alternatives before jumping to surgery?

And let's not overlook the nature of the treatments themselves— all of them were invasive:

- Baclofen pumps, surgically implanted in the spine to regulate muscle tone
- Dorsal rhizotomy, a procedure that involves cutting spinal nerves to reduce tightness
- Multiple orthopedic surgeries to force muscle lengthening in her legs

But here's the part that changed everything: We found a safe, noninvasive solution that actually worked—a circulation-boosting electrical stimulation device called Revitive. Anna simply placed her feet on it. No surgery. No drugs. No side effects—and it cost just $300. The results were better than we could have imagined—far more effective than all the invasive, high-risk procedures that had been pushed on us.

This isn't just about conflicting opinions; it's about a systemic flaw —how a fragmented, procedure-driven medical system misses the bigger picture. Anna's experience shows what happens when patients and families question the status quo and explore options beyond the invasive norm.

What's most frustrating is that the information about neuromuscular stimulation (NMS) wasn't hidden in some obscure medical journal—it was actually well documented and accessible. I discovered it while reading Dr. Norman Doidge's *The Brain's Way of Healing: Remarkable Discoveries and Recoveries from the Frontiers of Neuroplasticity* (2015). In this groundbreaking book, Dr. Doidge details how this technology was being successfully used throughout Europe and in research centers worldwide. The science was solid, the results were documented and clinicians in other countries were regularly employing these devices as first-line treatments rather than last resorts. Yet somehow, this knowledge hadn't penetrated American medical practice. Our specialists, sequestered in their narrowing fields of expertise, remained unaware of—or perhaps uninterested in—approaches outside their traditional toolkits. This wasn't just a gap in knowledge; it revealed a deeper flaw in how medical information flows in our healthcare system. Innovations that don't generate significant revenue for hospitals, don't show up in medical journal ads or don't fit neatly into existing billing codes rarely find their way into standard practice (regardless of their effectiveness). Anna's story isn't just about one device that worked—it's about how many other healing approaches might be sitting just outside the spotlight of conventional care, waiting to be discovered by determined patients and families willing to look beyond what they're told is possible.

And as always, the impact on me was huge. It made me stop and question—was I unintentionally following the same patterns with my own patients? Was I overlooking simple solutions in favor of standard protocols just because that's how I was trained? How could I take what I was learning and truly apply it to the people I was trying to help? And why weren't more doctors recommending these kinds of options that clearly worked? The answer became painfully clear: It lies in how doctors are trained—in silos—and how the entire medical system is structured to reward performing procedures over individualized care (we talked about this back in Chapter Six).

Fear and the Standard of Care

Another major issue? Doctors fear lawsuits.

From day one of medical school, I was warned: "Every patient is a potential lawsuit." The safest option is to follow standard protocols—because any deviation could put a doctor's career at risk.

I was told during my training:

- Be careful treating Lyme disease—too many antibiotics, and you could lose your license. It's not the standard of care.
- You can't take an autoimmune patient off their meds.
- If you step outside the guidelines, you could get sued.

The problem isn't what evidence-based medicine (EBM) was supposed to be; it is what it has become. Originally EBM had three pillars (Stony Brook University Libraries, 2025):

1. Up-to-date research
2. Physician's clinical experience
3. Patient preference

Today's system has dismissed patient preferences as irrelevant and relegated clinical experience to mere storytelling, creating an overreliance on industry-sponsored studies to drive medical decisions. And get this: **50 percent of published research findings are later proven false**—a shaky foundation for medicine.

This is one of the first and foundational principles I learned when I started my functional medicine training in 2010. It came from Dr. John Ioannidis' groundbreaking 2005 essay "Why Most Published Research Findings Are False," published in PLOS Medicine (Ioannidis, 2025). The essay shook the medical world by exposing a startling truth: Much of what we accept as scientific fact is, in reality, built on shaky ground. Ioannidis revealed that due to factors like small sample sizes, selective reporting, researcher bias and financial conflicts of interest, a majority of published medical research cannot be trusted at face value. This insight became a cornerstone of my approach to healthcare—instilling in me a relentless commitment to question conventional wisdom, dig deeper than surface-level studies and prioritize patient outcomes over rigid adherence to flawed data. It was the spark that drove me to challenge the assembly-line model of medicine and advocate for individualized, evidence-informed care that actually works.

But our defensive, liability-oriented healthcare culture leads to an overreliance on established protocols and invasive interventions. When combined with a payment structure that rewards physicians far more generously for performing procedures than for providing thoughtful, investigative care, the result is predictable—innovative, less-invasive approaches remain unexplored, while the status quo perpetuates itself unchallenged. Physicians are incentivized to follow the well-worn path rather than pioneering new ones, regardless of what might truly benefit the patient.

This is why Anna was offered aggressive medical interventions instead of noninvasive solutions that actually worked.

Finding Allies: Patient Advocacy Groups

Once you've identified systemic issues in your own healthcare experiences, the next step is to find allies who can help you navigate the complex medical maze. I used to mainly recommend patient advocacy groups as a powerful resource. They empower patients to question ineffective treatments, demand higher standards of care and steer clear of unnecessary procedures. But unfortunately, they often become echo chambers for disgruntled and mistreated patients. In the last year, I've discovered another invaluable set of allies: AI tools like Perplexity, Claude and ChatGPT. These platforms have become my go-to research companions—faster, more flexible and incredibly effective. (Of course this list changes weekly due to new updates, so when this book comes out this list will be obsolete.) They're especially helpful for cross-checking what you learn in online groups and for keeping you from falling into the same research rabbit holes that so many patients get stuck in. In many ways, I've found these tools even more useful than advocacy groups, because you can direct them to search only clinical research and skip over the massive wave of misinformation that exists online. I am even able to take complicated research articles, download them into the platform then use it to skim and summarize for me. Then I can ask questions and literally interact with the research articles. Another game changer that as of now is being left on the sidelines by our medical establishment.

Building Your Own Support Ecosystem

Once you've identified systemic issues in your healthcare experiences, the next step is to surround yourself with people who can help you navigate this complex world—without pulling you out of the ecosystem we're building together. You don't have to do this alone, and you shouldn't. Human connection and trust are essential, and while outside groups can be helpful, the goal here is to empower you from within this community.

Begin by exploring the comprehensive library of resources I've carefully built over the past decade specifically for this purpose. In my quest to educate people, since 2016 I have been consolidating a wide range of educational materials. I've organized research, translated complex medical concepts into accessible language and developed actionable frameworks for various health challenges. Over the years, I've vetted more than 400 books, authored over 300 blogs and helped develop a library of more than 1000 video and audio resources. Our website will lead you to all these materials (**Aaron-HartmanMD.com**), or access resources using the QR code at the end of each chapter. You could even use AI to search the entire library to find exactly what you want, super quick. (One moonshot goal is to have an AI version of me and all my work available for people to ask questions. When available, you will find it on my website as well.) Rather than wandering through the unvetted wilderness of online information, you'll find trusted, evidence-based guidance tailored to your condition within our educational platform. Whether you're dealing with autoimmune issues, chronic fatigue, gut disorders or unexplained symptoms, you'll find dedicated sections addressing your specific concerns. For those with rare conditions who have faced medical dismissal, I've created specialized resources drawn from both clinical research and the lived experiences of patients who've successfully navigated these challenges. Everything is designed with one goal: empowering you with knowledge that conventional healthcare often fails to provide. This isn't random information—it's a carefully curated pathway to becoming your own best advocate.

Within my extensive library, you'll find a wealth of carefully curated resources developed over the past decade to empower your healthcare journey:

Comprehensive guides on navigating the healthcare system through our blog series and podcast episodes that explain your rights as a patient and how to effectively assert them when facing resistance

Expert-created resources on specific health conditions spanning everything from hormonal imbalances and autoimmune conditions to mold illness and gut health—organized by category so you can quickly find information relevant to your specific concerns

The "Made for Health" podcast and video resources feature practical strategies for preparing for medical appointments, asking the right questions and ensuring your concerns are addressed, even with the most time-constrained providers

These resources have been refined through my more than 25 years of clinical experience seeing what actually works for real patients facing real healthcare obstacles. Rather than piecing together advice from scattered internet sources of questionable quality, you'll find everything organized in one trustworthy location—continuously updated as medical understanding evolves.

This space is designed to be your container—to help you filter external resources, make sense of them and apply them in ways that serve your unique journey. We're here to walk with you, not just point you somewhere else.

Become an Informed Healthcare Consumer

Let's explore the foundational principles of functional medicine —the framework that revolutionized my approach to healing. This isn't your usual WebMD search. We're going deep, folks. Start by grabbing a book or two. Dr. Richard Bland's *The Disease Delusion* is a solid pick. Commonly known as the "father of functional medicine," he walks readers through the errors in how our current healthcare system approaches care and dives into the basics of functional medicine. As you read, jot down what stands out. Note the differences from regular medicine. Next, hit the web. But don't just go looking anywhere. I have been working on compiling the ultimate online resource list for over 10 years, and we have over 300 blogs on topics from hormones and gut health to chronic fatigue, POTS and autoimmune hacks. This is a gold mine of info. Don't just skim—really dig in. Read stories, watch videos and listen to podcasts. The goal is to learn how functional medicine views your body as one big, connected system. If you are overwhelmed by it, you could always use your friendly AI tool to scan and review the site for information. (Again, check to see if my Aaron Hartman, MD AI is available because then you can just ask your questions.) Or start with my intro series, *Foundations of Functional Medicine*.

Learn, think, incorporate and act!

This isn't about becoming a doctor. It's about getting the basics so you can make smart health choices. Think of your research like learning a new language—the language of your body and how it works with the world around you. At first, it's incomprehensible and seems like gibberish, but over time, you start to understand bits and pieces, say words and sentences and eventually you become fluent in the language, and it becomes your mother tongue.

Now, let's talk about using holistic thinking for your own health issues. This is where the rubber meets the road. Start by stepping back and looking at the big picture of your health. Instead of focusing on one symptom, try to see how everything might be connected.

Let's say you get headaches a lot. In the old way, you might just pop a pill. But in a holistic way, you'd think about your food, your stress, your sleep, your environment—even your relationships. Maybe those headaches come from tension in your neck from bad posture at work. Or maybe certain foods set them off. It could be they go away on the weekends (when you are out of your moldy school or workplace) or get better when you are on vacation (related to mold in your home), or maybe they are caused by a simple magnesium deficiency.

To think holistically, keep a detailed health journal (we talked about this in the last chapter). Write down not just your symptoms, but what you eat, how you sleep, your stress levels and anything else that might matter. Over time, you might see patterns. Maybe your headaches always show up after eating certain foods, or during stressful times at work. Maybe they go away on weekends (when you're out of your moldy school or workplace) or when on vacation (your moldy home).

Next, think about how different parts of your life might affect your health. Consider if you're moving enough. Evaluate your work-life balance. Reflect on your relationships—whether they lift you up or drag you down. Remember, in holistic thinking, everything's connected. That fight with your partner might be messing with your sleep, which could be hurting your immune system.

Do your homework: Research your conditions, treatments and providers. While you shouldn't try to replace medical expertise, informed patients get better care.

Seek multiple opinions: For significant diagnoses or procedures, especially those involving substantial risk, get second opinions from practitioners with different training backgrounds.

Ask for time: Don't be rushed into major decisions. Take time to carefully consider what has been recommended and allow extra time if needed for additional consultations.

Bring support: Having an advocate with you during important medical visits can help ensure your questions are answered and your concerns are addressed.

Record your health visits: I routinely recommend that my patients record our visits so that they can go back and listen to it for a second time to pick up things they may have missed. I also recommend that they turn it into a transcript that they can put into an AI tool to summarize our conversation—and to even ask questions like *"What does this mean?"* or *"Clarify these topics."*

Build Your Healthcare Team

Find a primary care provider who listens: Look for someone who takes time to understand your health goals and concerns, not just manage your diseases. In today's age that would be a functional medicine provider who has experience in both conventional medicine and integrative/functional medicine.

Consider integrative approaches: Practitioners trained in both conventional and functional medicine can often provide more comprehensive care.

Maintain your own health records: Keep copies of all test results, imaging studies and treatment notes. You may need this information when working with new providers.

Stay engaged: Your health is too important to delegate completely to others, no matter how qualified they may be.

Trust, but verify: The proverb "trust, but verify" applies perfectly to healthcare. Trust your healthcare providers' expertise and intentions, but verify their recommendations through:

- Independent research
- Second opinions
- Your own experience and intuition
- Tracking your responses to treatments

By now you probably feel a bit more confident in your ability to navigate appointments, diagnoses, treatments and the feeling of isolation that often comes with health challenges. Now, let's take it a step further—let's get armed with specific questions to take with you into the exam room, and how to be the leader in your care plan. However, if you are feeling overwhelmed, then no worries. We have created Connected Health just for you. You'll learn more about it below.

Scan the QR code below with your phone's camera. This will direct you to open a web page that provides instant access to our comprehensive collection of free resources.

9

TAKING CONTROL OF YOUR TREATMENT

T aking control of your healthcare isn't just about reading more or asking better questions—it's about radically shifting how you view your role in the medical system. Anna's story didn't unfold the way it did by chance. It happened because we challenged the system at every turn. We replaced fear with facts, passivity with persistence and blind obedience with clear-eyed, critical thinking. That's the real blueprint.

So if you've ever felt steamrolled by rushed appointments, pressured into procedures or dismissed for asking "too many questions," know this: You're not alone—and you're not powerless.

Start by peering beneath the surface of your own medical experiences. Spot the patterns. Identify the system's blind spots. When you face a new recommendation, pause. Ask, "Is this truly the only way?" Because if a $300 electrical stimulation device could replace invasive surgeries for Anna, then other overlooked solutions might exist for you too.

You don't need a medical degree to reclaim ownership of your health—you need guts, strategy and the willingness to question everything. You are not a passive recipient of care. You are the lead decision-maker. So stay sharp. Speak up. Challenge assumptions.

Because nobody is more qualified to fight for your well-being than you are.

Assertive Communication: Standing Your Ground in Medical Settings

Doctors are often rushed and overworked, which can make it difficult for patients to get the attention they deserve. But remember —you are the expert on your own body, and your concerns matter.

Tips for Speaking Up:

- **Be direct.** Instead of saying, "I don't know about this treatment," try, "I'm concerned about the side effects. Are there alternatives?"
- **Use confident body language.** Sit up straight, maintain eye contact and speak in a steady voice.
- **Be persistent if necessary.** If a doctor dismisses your concerns, say, "I know you're busy, but I need to discuss this further before making a decision."
- **Come prepared.** Write your questions down, keep a journal and stay on top of the answers you get from each practitioner (more on journaling later in Chapter 17).
- **Be willing to make multiple follow-up appointments.** You likely won't get all your questions answered in one visit due to time constraints, so you need to be willing to set up multiple visits asking two to three questions at a time. This shows a mutual respect for the practitioner's time constraints. Communicate to them that you are doing this *because* you respect their time!
- **Bring a support person.** A friend or family member can help reinforce your concerns and take notes.

Anna's case shows how crucial it is to push back against medical pressure. Initially we were told she *had* to undergo surgery. Not doing it wasn't an option. But by taking a pause, speaking up and looking for other answers, we found other solutions—and she has thrived.

Questions Lead to Better Health Outcomes and Can Save Your Life

One of the biggest flaws in modern medicine is the assumption that doctors always know best. But as Anna's case proves, blindly following recommendations can lead to unnecessary and harmful interventions.

When it comes to asking questions when you're in front of your provider, it's normal to feel nervous. Coming in prepared with a list of questions helps, but an acronym that patients find really helpful in these situations is "BRAIN":

Benefits: What are the benefits of this procedure
or treatment?
Risks: What are the risks associated with the procedure
or treatment?
Alternatives: Are there any alternatives to this recommendation?
Intuition: What is my intuition telling me about this treatment, next step or doctor?
Nothing: What if I do nothing instead of this treatment? Can I wait? What happens if I delay or refuse this treatment? What is the worst thing that could happen if I don't go through with it?

Developing the habit of asking critical questions is crucial. Here are a few more questions to keep in your back pocket:

- What exactly is this treatment, and how does it work?
- How does this fit into my overall health plan?
- Do you have other patients who have had success with this recommendation? If so, can you tell me about their experience?

We asked these questions every step of the way. When doctors recommended surgeries, we asked, "Is there a less invasive way to achieve the same goal?" These questions led to solutions like the electrical stimulation therapy mentioned earlier—a noninvasive approach that prevented major surgeries.

Then after all of that ask yourself the question, "Is this truly the best option I have at this time, and if we delay this therapy what can we do in its place?" Remember, you were made for health. Your body was designed to self-heal and self-repair. You are just attempting to give your body what it needs to do what it was made to do.

Asking your medical provider questions like the ones suggested above is critical for several reasons—all of which contribute to better health outcomes and strengthen the patient-provider relationship, thereby improving your individualized health plan:

Improved understanding and clarity: We've all been overwhelmed by medical language, and you want to understand exactly what is being recommended in terms that make sense to you. A lot of doctors don't realize they're speaking another language when they throw out words they use every day, so you can bridge that knowledge gap by asking for clarification to be sure you understand exactly what you're agreeing to—or refusing.

Informed decision-making: You want to understand your condition, the pros and cons of treatment options and what to expect from tests or procedures. Becoming informed empowers you to make decisions about your own care to be sure it aligns with your values and preferences. Think of this as "shared decision-making."

Enhanced safety: Medical errors arise when there is miscommunication. Don't be shy about needing clarification with things like instructions or verifying the medication dosages—this reduces the risk of mistakes.

Personalized care: Your doctor may know a lot about medicine, but they don't know everything about *you*. Your questions provide valuable insights into your lifestyle, concerns, priorities and how your condition affects your daily life. This helps your doctor tailor a treatment plan that truly meets your individual needs.

Building trust: Being an engaged patient and asking questions shows that you are invested in your health. This fosters a stronger, more collaborative relationship built on trust and mutual respect, which can lead to better communication and a more positive health-care experience.

Empowering yourself: Asking questions shifts you from a passive recipient of care to an active participant in your health journey. This empowerment allows you to feel more in control and confident in managing your health, ultimately leading to improved outcomes.

The right questions can cut through medical complexity and help you get better care. Good healthcare providers welcome informed patients and thoughtful questions. Here are the most important questions I've learned to ask—both as a physician and as a patient advocate:

Before Any Treatment or Procedure

What is this treatment supposed to accomplish? Get specific goals, not vague promises. "This should help" isn't good enough.

What are the risks and potential side effects? Every intervention carries risks. Make sure you understand them fully.

What happens if we wait? Sometimes the best treatment is no treatment. Understand the consequences of delaying intervention.

Are there less invasive alternatives? Many conditions can be treated through lifestyle changes, nutrition or other approaches before resorting to drugs or surgery.

How will we measure success? Without clear metrics, you can't determine if treatments are working.

For Chronic Conditions

What's causing this condition? If your doctor can only describe what you have but not why you have it, they may be missing root causes.

How does this connect to other symptoms? Your body is an integrated system. Isolated treatments for seemingly unrelated symptoms may miss important connections. If they don't see this connection, it might be time for another provider.

What can I do to support my body's natural healing? Beyond medical treatments, what lifestyle factors could help or hurt your recovery?

Have you seen patients with similar conditions improve significantly? Experience with successful outcomes suggests a practitioner who understands how to help your condition and navigate through the rough patches you may encounter.

For Diagnostic Tests

What are you looking for with this test? Understanding the purpose helps you evaluate whether the test is necessary.

How will the results change my treatment? If test results won't influence treatment decisions, the test may be unnecessary.

What are the risks of this test? Even diagnostic procedures can carry risks that should be weighed against benefits.

Are there alternative ways to get this information? Sometimes less invasive or expensive tests can provide similar information.

Red Flag Responses

Be cautious if healthcare providers respond to your questions with:

- Defensiveness or irritation
- "Don't worry about that"
- "Just trust me"
- "You wouldn't understand"
- "That's not how we do things here"

I have a powerful resource that could be a real game changer for you—it's called "How to Talk to Your Doctor." My team created it specifically to guide you through the thought process and actionable steps of organizing what you've learned, and then presenting that information to your healthcare provider in a way that fosters a true collaborative team dynamic. It's more than just a guide—it's a roadmap to becoming an empowered patient who actively shapes their care. You can access it via the QR code below, and I strongly encourage you to take full advantage of it.

I hope this chapter has helped you feel more empowered as a patient—after all, your medical practitioners are working for you! Keep reading to learn about how to advocate for yourself and others, and how to interpret good information from bad when it comes to doing your own research.

Scan the QR code below with your phone's camera. This will direct you to open a web page that provides instant access to our comprehensive collection of free resources.

10

ADVOCACY

Dealing with chronic conditions like Anna's cerebral palsy is tough. But what's even tougher? Navigating a healthcare system that prioritizes protocols over people. Being a good advocate isn't just important—it's essential. This chapter will help you learn how to be a better advocate, make smart choices, stay strong and explore alternative treatments. By the end, you'll possess the confidence, knowledge and strategic approach needed to transform from passive patient to empowered navigator of a system that wasn't designed for nuance or personalized care.

The Reality of Advocacy

The key to being a strong advocate is unwavering determination paired with true informed consent, not the shell of consent our system adheres to. For Anna, our advocacy began not with blind trust in specialists, but with critical evaluation of every recommendation. As discussed, start by creating your own evaluation system—a mental checklist that asks whether the intervention is truly necessary, what are the alternatives and what happens if we wait? This approach saved Anna from multiple surgeries presented as inevitable.

Build your knowledge fortress that empowers you to confidently advocate for yourself or your loved one. I spent countless early mornings researching cerebral palsy, brain development and neuroplasticity—not just from conventional medical journals but from outlier research, international approaches and practitioners working at the boundaries of healing. This diversity of information became my greatest weapon when specialists presented limited options. For Anna, this meant discovering neuromuscular stimulation when others recommended spinal cord surgery. Your journey will have different specifics, but the principle remains: The parent or patient who knows more than the average doctor about their specific condition becomes impossible to dismiss—and your knowledge is your superpower.

When it comes to engaging with doctors, always be respectful—but don't be afraid to be assertive. Come to every appointment with a written list of questions, but not too many. If something doesn't make sense or feels rushed, ask for clarification. Repeat back what you understand to confirm alignment. The healthcare system values speed, not depth—so it's up to you to push for clarity and thoroughness. And when your appointment time is over, be respectful of the practitioner's time but schedule a follow-up appointment on your way out so you can continue down your list of questions.

And finally, document everything. During every visit, take notes on what was discussed, decisions made and the next steps. After the visit, review your notes and write a summary. Keep a timeline. This not only helps you stay organized—it ensures continuity of care and empowers you to remain in control, even as the system tries to move too fast or forgets key details.

I wish we'd had even a fraction of the resources that are available today back when we were going through it. In 2006, functional medicine was still labeled as quackery, and the idea that food could impact health was laughed at. So much has changed since then—but back then, we had to figure it all out ourselves. It took us nearly two years just to learn how to properly source the food our daughter needed—

two years! But today, you don't have to go through that. We've already done the hard work and this resource is available to you on our resource page. Please, let this book and everything inside it fast-track your healing process. That's the reason we created this—it's why we're doing all of this. Because you are worth it. (Be sure to scan the QR code at the end of this chapter to find our free Food Sourcing Guide.)

Making Smart Healthcare Choices

Anna's journey took a drastically different path because we refused to accept the status quo. Instead of blindly following recommendations for feeding tubes, unnecessary surgeries and pharmaceutical fixes, we opted for real food, holistic therapies, functional neurology, lipid therapy and gait analysis. The result? A thriving 19-year-old who beat and exceeded every expectation.

You must take the same approach—seeing doctors as partners, not authorities. When a doctor suggests a treatment, ask about the evidence behind it. Does it truly work? You'll be surprised to learn that many of the recommended therapies don't actually work that well.

The standard medical model is broken because it treats symptoms instead of addressing root causes. This is why 40 percent of Americans are insulin resistant ("Trends in Hyperinsulinemia and Insulin Resistance Among Nondiabetic US Adults, NHANES, 1999–2018," Wu et al., 2025), one in 31 children now has autism ("Data and Statistics on Autism Spectrum Disorder," Center for Disease Control, 2025) and millions suffer from chronic conditions like Lyme disease, autoimmune disorders and gastrointestinal issues. Yet instead of evolving, the system maintains its outdated approach:

1. A patient presents symptoms.
2. A doctor prescribes medication, a procedure or a specialist referral.
3. The patient moves on—until symptoms worsen.

This system is not much different from the one my grandfather had to navigate over 50 years ago. Yes, we have a lot more cool tech, but the delivery system is not that much different. Think about that for a moment.

The problem? This method works for acute issues like heart attacks, infections or broken bones. We are actually the best in the world for acute care issues—this is why people travel from all over the world for treatment. But we fail miserably when it comes to treating complex, chronic illnesses.

Instead of accepting the first option given, explore alternatives. Seek second opinions—not just from other doctors, but also from nutritionists, physical therapists and functional medicine practitioners. Consider treatments that address underlying imbalances, like dietary changes, gut health and sleep optimization and then integrate in additional therapies like hyperbaric oxygen therapy.

Staying Strong Through the Challenges

Being an advocate is exhausting. The system will wear you down, making it easy to surrender and just take the default path of least resistance. But resilience is key. Here are some reminders of how to stay strong and resist returning to being a passive patient:

- Start by allowing yourself to feel your emotions. It's okay to be scared or frustrated. Writing your thoughts in a journal can help process them.
- See every challenge as an opportunity for growth. Every hurdle is a chance to better understand the system and find new solutions.
- Set small goals and celebrate each success, no matter how minor. Every step forward adds up (read *Tiny Habits: The Small Changes That Change Everything,* Fogg, 2020).
- Look back at your gains and see how far you have come. This one mindset change can radically alter your perspective on your healing journey (read *The Gap and the*

Gain: The High Achievers' Guide to Happiness, Confidence, and Success, Sullivan and Hardy, 2021).

- Surround yourself with a strong support team—family, friends and medical professionals who genuinely care. The average complex patient gets shuffled between myriads of different specialists, none of whom coordinate care. But you can build a team that puts your needs first.

- Find ways to manage stress, like deep breathing, yoga or even short walks. Taking care of yourself is just as important as advocating for your loved one. (We have put together an entire course just on this topic of dealing with stress and trauma. Use the QR code at the end of this chapter for access to our mini trauma course from Connected Health).

A great concept to integrate here I learned from reading *The Gap and The Gain* by Benjamin Hardy: Stop looking ahead to the horizon, a false destination that you will never reach. Horizons are illusions. Our human nature always propels our goals forward as we make progress. Instead, look back at where you have come from. That puts your progress into perspective.

And most importantly, remind yourself daily why you're fighting. For us, it was Anna—her smile, her spirit, her potential. We were reminded of our "why" every single day, and that purpose became our fuel. Without it, the weight of appointments, decisions and setbacks might have crushed us. But when you know exactly who or what you're fighting for, your resolve becomes unshakable. Anna's success wasn't a fluke—it was built on years of relentless persistence, anchored by a crystal-clear sense of purpose. Your journey may be long, uncertain and at times overwhelming, but when your "why" is front and center, the fight becomes more than manageable—it becomes meaningful. And it's worth it!

Exploring Alternative Treatments

TRADITIONAL MEDICINE HAD a blueprint for Anna: surgeries, feeding tubes and pharmaceuticals. But by stepping outside that model, she was able to thrive. The same potential exists for others facing complex, chronic conditions—if you're willing to look beyond the status quo.

Start by researching alternative therapies that are specific to your condition. Look for practitioners of integrative or functional medicine—physicians who see the entire person, not just isolated symptoms. Functional medicine is about getting to the root cause, not just putting a Band-Aid on the pain.

Choose therapies that offer high reward with low risk. Lipid therapy can support brain function. Hyperbaric oxygen therapy shows promise in neurological healing. Peptides activate your body's natural healing pathways. And never underestimate the power of food —nutritional interventions alone can shift the trajectory for conditions like autoimmune diseases, gut disorders and chronic fatigue.

Supplements and micronutrients may seem like a simplistic solution, but many chronic conditions stem from deficiencies that traditional medicine often overlooks. Always work with a knowledgeable provider before adding anything new to your routine.

Other powerful options? Look into acupuncture for nervous system regulation, craniosacral and fascial release work to support alignment, calm the nervous system and improve lymphatic flow, massage for muscular and emotional relief and trauma-informed brain retraining to help reset the body's stress patterns.

Newer cutting-edge therapies like exosomes and stem cells can be super helpful for certain musculoskeletal conditions as well as for regenerative medicine biohacks. These kinds of therapies harness the healing potential your body had when you were younger. In certain situations, they can be amazing add-ons after you've gotten all the basics down.

The medical path Anna was given was paved with limitations. But the one she walked—rooted in curiosity, persistence and holistic care —opened doors no traditional protocol ever could.

Healing is possible. You just have to be willing to ask a different set of questions and explore alternative solutions.

Anna's success isn't unique—it's just rare because so few people dare to defy the system. But here's the truth: You can do this too. This is the turning point—the moment you realize that what once felt impossible is actually within reach. You don't need to be extraordinary; you just need to be willing to challenge the status quo, ask hard questions and refuse to settle for "standard" care when your gut says there's a better way.

Trust Your Instincts—The Science Behind Gut Feelings

There is a crucial aspect of advocacy that deserves special mention: following your gut instincts. In traditional medicine, this is often dismissed as unscientific "woo-woo" or baseless fantasy. Yet cutting-edge neuroscience research reveals that our intuition—that visceral gut feeling—plays a fundamental role in our brain's decision-making process. Jonathan Haidt, in his illuminating book *The Righteous Mind*, explains this phenomenon using a powerful metaphor: Your conscious mind is like a rider atop an elephant, while your subconscious intuition is the elephant itself. The elephant does the bulk of the work and preliminary decision-making, with the final executive choice confirmed by your conscious mind. Malcolm Gladewell talks about a similar concept in his book *Blink: The Power of Thinking Without Thinking*.

What does this mean for you as a patient, parent or advocate? Those moments when something feels wrong about a treatment plan, when a specialist's recommendation doesn't sit right or when you sense there must be another option—these aren't just emotional reactions to be dismissed. They're your sophisticated neurological system processing millions of data points beneath your awareness. Science now confirms what parents like us have always known:

Intuition has a biological basis and should never be ignored, especially when advocating for someone you love.

By practicing strong advocacy, making informed choices, staying resilient and exploring new treatments, you take back control of your health—or your child's. You stop being a passive recipient of care and become the leader of your health journey. Yes, the system wasn't built for healing, but that doesn't mean you have to be trapped by its limitations.

Be curious. Stay relentless. Keep questioning everything; listen to your gut instincts. You're no longer just surviving in the system—you're rewriting the path forward. Every time you listen to and trust your intuition, you sharpen it and hone your ability to hear it. Your health journey is yours, and now you know: You have the power to shape it. I know I keep using the word "journey," but that's because it's your life, your health and it's unique to you and your needs—it's up to you to design the map and navigate your way through it.

Scan the QR code below with your phone's camera. This will direct you to open a web page that provides instant access to our comprehensive collection of free resources.

PART III

A NEW APPROACH

FUNCTIONAL MEDICINE AND ROOT-CAUSE HEALING

11

FAITH MEETS MEDICINE

Our journey with Anna didn't just change her life—it transformed our entire family and approach to health and healing. Up until the time we brought Anna home, I had been compartmentalizing—there was my medical career and work with patients, and there was my life with my wife, then caring for my family. Then there was our community—including our church. I have always been a man of faith, and I got into my profession because I felt a calling to be of service. That calling intensified when we brought Anna home, and writing this book is an extension of that calling.

How I navigated the system to get Anna the care she needed felt like a seismic shift in my perception and my faith. I could no longer compartmentalize my work, being a father and my faith—they needed to integrate. They were three pieces to the same puzzle: my life's purpose. I had to switch some things around to make sure they all fit together.

If you feel like something's missing in your healthcare and that the puzzle pieces don't fit, you're not alone. Many people find themselves stuck between conventional medicine and their beliefs. There is a way to bridge that gap. A new approach that mixes faith and science to heal the whole you. Let's incorporate this new approach into your life.

When you're sick, you visit the doctor, explain your symptoms, hopefully receive an accurate diagnosis and are sent on your way with a prescription or instructions that you typically follow in hopes of feeling and getting better as quickly as possible. But sometimes you may have underlying conditions that are difficult to diagnose, hidden symptoms or seemingly unrelated weird "things" going on that you don't think are relevant—and if your doctor doesn't think to ask, you probably won't think to share. For some, this means living in pain or discomfort, never truly healing from what is actually ailing them. This chapter digs into how changing what you think about health can actually help you heal.

It's like standing at a crossroads, staring down two very different paths. One is the well-worn road of traditional medicine—doctor visits, prescriptions and familiar protocols. The other is uncharted territory, where you take an active role, explore alternative approaches and dive deep into understanding your own body, your environment, your lifestyle and how they're all related.

But here's the thing—these two paths aren't mutually exclusive. The real magic happens when you blend both. When you trust medical expertise while also questioning, researching and experimenting with what truly works for you. Healing isn't just about following orders; it's about becoming *the expert* on yourself.

I also remind all of my patients that healing isn't linear. The path to health and wellness is a lot like the trajectory of the stock market —they're both unpredictable rides with highs and lows. But both are journeys of investment and are complex systems that are influenced by environmental factors. You might have a few weeks where you're up, experiencing progress, then a stressful event or dietary slip will set you back, making you feel like you've lost all your gains. So how do you maintain your sanity and emotional wellness through all these peaks and valleys?

I would like to talk about what faith means within the context of healthcare and wellness. Some people put their faith in medicine, in doctors or in science—so-called tangible things. Others put their faith in a Higher Power that gives their life purpose and meaning—so-called invisible things. But faith can be something even bigger.

Because of my faith, I know there are answers even if I don't have them quite yet. I know there's hope, even in the most hopeless situation. And I know the reality of my existence is much greater than anything that I can perceive with my senses. The world of science-based medicine, on the other hand, relies 100 percent on only what can be sensed: seen, touched and experienced. But even science teaches us that most of the reality of our universe is unseen. The light spectrum (visible light) represents a small fraction of the entire light spectrum. The same thing for sounds—we can only hear a fraction of what is in the spectrum of sounds. We even have to deploy special telescopes outside of the Earth's atmosphere to observe things we are unable to see due to limitations imposed by our eyes within our atmosphere. There is a disconnect between what we call science, what actual science is and what it shows us. The universe itself is expanding at the speed of light. How can our minds even comprehend that concept?

For me, faith gives me solid ground to stand on when I don't have all the facts to back that up. It gives me the ability to hope for a future that the current circumstances say is impossible. This is why when Becky said Anna was going to be okay (even though I had no idea what that meant), I brought her into my home and made her my daughter. It's the reason we didn't follow those specialist recommendations to put a feeding tube into her because it just didn't *feel* right. It wasn't for six more months that we found out the reason *why* it wasn't right. Hell, it's the reason I put up a shingle for my practice, not really expecting much to come of it (but my wife knew that it would blow up). People were looking for someone who would take the sum total of their scientific knowledge and medical expertise and not be limited by it, but use it as a light to shine in the dark places. To create hope for outcomes that weren't expected.

In her book *Sudden Death,* civil rights campaigner and feminist writer Rita Mae Brown said, "Insanity is doing the same thing over and over again and expecting different results" (a quote that is often misattributed to Albert Einstein). That's what our current healthcare system does: the same thing over and over again hoping for a different outcome. My faith enabled me to use everything I'd learned, everything I'd read and every patient I had seen to force me to look for things outside of my then-current realm of experience.

And this gives people hope. People who don't know what's going on with them—why their gut aches, why they feel dizzy or why they have brain fog. Or they had a cancer diagnosis and the chemotherapy wrecked their body. Or they want to make sure the cancer doesn't come back...or whatever. They want to know someone's going to fight for them and not give up. Someone's going to research and learn and take the entirety of that experience and apply it to them personally. People want a warrior, someone who's literally going to hop into the fray and swing the battle axe and fight for them. And you can't offer that unless you've done it first for yourself or your family.

Faith is not just believing in a higher power—it's living with the expectation that this higher power will show up and change lives. I came to this realization when Anna came into my life, and it was profound. Through trying to meet her medical needs and exceed the limited expectations the medical industry had for her, I realized that Anna was made for something greater than her diagnoses and treatments. She wasn't made for illness; she was made for health. That belief alone pushed me to work harder, never give up and expect the unexpected. And if I can believe that about someone with so many challenges, you can believe it about yourself.

I personally pray a mantra every morning on my drive to work: *Let me see what can't be seen, hear what can't be heard and diagnose what can't be diagnosed.* And you know what? It works—over and over again. I routinely notice things I'd previously overlooked—and too often to be chalked up to coincidence, I'll come across new information—an article, a treatment or a case study—just weeks before meeting a patient who's dealing with that exact condition and could benefit from what I've just learned. It's almost as if the answers are already out there, waiting to be recognized—if only we're willing to look beyond the obvious. When you open yourself to new possibilities, when you refuse to let conventional limitations define your health, you begin to notice solutions that others overlook.

My patient Sarah—I told you about her back in Chapter Three—was trapped in a relentless cycle of illness. For several years, she followed her doctor's instructions faithfully, taking medications and adhering to traditional treatments. But instead of improving, her condition worsened and she found herself sinking deeper into exhaustion and frustration. Desperate for answers, she took matters into her own hands. She combed through research, joined online communities and experimented with alternative approaches like meditation and brain retraining—hoping and praying for a breakthrough and to be healed. But nothing worked.

Deep down, she refused to believe that this was the end of the road. She *knew* there were answers out there—she just hadn't found them yet. She had faith that she would, and relied on that faith to keep her motivated. And then after relentless searching, she discovered my website and online community. That's when everything changed. She dove in headfirst, arming herself with knowledge and connecting with others who were on the same journey. She eventually uncovered the shocking cause of her illness: Mold was silently sabotaging her health.

Once she recognized the root cause of her suffering, she didn't hesitate to make every change required. She overhauled her diet, made bold lifestyle changes and ultimately left her mold-infested home. The results were almost immediate. Her body responded with newfound energy, her brain fog and mind cleared and for the first time in years, she felt *alive* again.

Sarah's journey wasn't just about finding the right treatment—it was about refusing to accept the limitations and blind spots in healthcare. She didn't wait for a doctor or a scientific expert to hand her incomplete answers—she went looking for them herself. And that's the lesson: Healing isn't always mapped out for you by someone else. Sometimes, you have to keep searching—even when you don't know *exactly* what you're searching for. Because the answers are out there. And, like Sarah, sometimes you need to be empowered by faith to search and find them.

My family and I are Christian, but faith isn't just about religion, and faith doesn't mean ignoring doctors and relying on prayer. It means believing in something greater—your own body's natural ability to heal, your inner strength, a Higher Power and the unexpected ways recovery can unfold. True faith is not just wishful thinking; it's the quiet confidence that healing is possible, even when the way forward isn't clear. As the Bible gently reminds us, faith is "confidence in what we hope for and assurance about what we do not see" (Hebrews, 11:1). Faith is about trusting that answers are out there, even if they haven't revealed themselves yet, and continuing to seek them with an open and hopeful heart.

So how do you start? First, think about what you believe about health. Write it down. Then, ask yourself if those beliefs are always true. For example, if you think doctors always know best, remember times when you were right about your own body without a doctor being involved—times you listened to your body and took a nap, drank more water or went for a walk. On the other hand, if you believe doctors don't know anything and that only natural remedies work, think about times when medical treatments actually helped you or someone you love recover—think of all of the cancer patients who are still alive, children who have received a lung transplant or premature babies being kept alive in the NICU. The key is this: to challenge your assumptions and stay open to both possibilities.

Next, get curious about your health. Ask questions. Why this treatment? Are there other options? Staying curious can teach you a lot about your body. Remember, working with doctors also involves using all parts of yourself—body, mind and spirit—to get better. It's a collaboration.

You might feel scared to question things about your health. That's okay. But remember, every big medical discovery started with someone asking questions. A great way to feel more confident is to talk to other people doing the same thing. Join groups online or in your area. If you can't find one you trust, join ours. But you can never give up and accept the status quo.

Don't be afraid to try new kinds of doctors too. Some people feel better when they mix regular medicine with other kinds of treatments. You could see a naturopathic doctor along with your regular one for natural healing options. Or try something like acupuncture for pain. See a myofascial or massage specialist to help your body to relax. Or a medical doctor trained in functional medicine to help tie all these things together. Or a precision medicine physician to get a super individualized health optimization plan. In medicine, this is called a multidisciplinary approach—and you are part of the medical team. The most important part! Just keep an open mind and pay attention to how you feel.

Now how does your faith fit with your health? It's all in the choices you make. First ask yourself, what is your *Why*? *Why* do you need your health and want to get better? What do you believe about health and healing? Do you believe you were made for health and being sick just isn't the way things are supposed to be? Are you a part of something greater and believe a Higher Power plays a role in your health? Do you believe there is something out there for you but you just haven't found it yet? Or maybe your health issues are keeping you from fulfilling your life's purpose. Reflect on whether you see your body as something sacred to care for. Or if you believe your mindset can help your physical health.

Once you have identified your beliefs, think about how they might guide your health choices. If you believe in prayer, you might add it to your healing routine. If community is important, you might join support groups or faith-based wellness programs.

Think about how your faith might guide what you eat. Many religions have rules about food—like fasting, not eating certain meats or eating whole, natural foods. Consider how these might fit with the functional medicine stuff you've been learning. One of the books on our reading list, *Blue Zones* by Dan Buettner, discusses a community of Seventh-Day Adventists in Southern California and how their lifestyle of a plant-based diet combined with exercise and social activities makes them one of the longest-living groups in the world.

Get creative in mixing spiritual practices with your healing routine. This could be as simple as starting your day by saying thanks, or as big as going on a faith-based wellness retreat. The key is to find practices that feel right to you and support your health goals.

Remember, this isn't about replacing medical care with faith stuff. It's about mixing the two to support your whole self—body, mind and spirit. You might find your faith gives you strength to stick with a tough treatment plan, or that your spiritual practices help lower stress and boost healing. Simon Sinek, David Mead and Peter Docker wrote a book called *Find Your Why* that outlines this process from a different perspective. Victor Frankl's book, *Man's Search for Meaning,* is all about the concept that if you know your *Why* you can endure almost any circumstance. Your faith and belief system is more powerful than you can possibly imagine.

Your *How* is about the specific behaviors, processes and methods you use to fulfill that purpose. The final, tangible outcome of your efforts is your *What*.

As you change how you think about health, you might start changing other parts of your life too. You might speak up more or notice more about how your body feels. That's because when you start asking questions in one area, it's easy to do it in others. Once you advocate for yourself in one area of your life, it becomes a natural instinct in every other area.

Now, let's talk about tangible actions you can take. Start by researching your condition beyond conventional sources. This doesn't mean ignoring your doctor; it means learning more on top of what you're being told. Let's be honest–in a quick ten-minute doctor's visit, there is just only so much you can talk about. You have to get educated and involved in your own healthcare.

Use good websites with reputable sources, medical books and journals to learn about your health problem and ways to treat it. Keep notes on what you find. These days, AI can be a great tool with which to scour the web for ideas or information and for taking deep dives.

When you're doing your own research, be careful about where you get your info. Look for original studies and references, not just blog posts or Reddit threads. Check credentials on authors—an influencer is not an expert, and they may just be trying to sell you supplements. Augment all the information you are gathering with stories from people with the same problem as you who are getting better and healing (avoid any site where people are just complaining in a vacuum and aren't willing to try a new approach: This is the exact opposite of what we want).

Next, think about joining patient communities where others are dealing with the same kind of health problems. These can be great places to get support, troubleshoot and learn new ideas. When you join, start by reading what others say. Then, when you're ready, ask questions and share your own story. However, I always warn people about these groups because sometimes they are just places for negative people who aren't getting better to air out their complaints and grievances. So finding the right ones is key, as is weighing everything you learn with your personal journey and the medical advice you're receiving. That is why for this step, ideally, you would be working with a functional medicine doctor. It can keep you from going down the wrong path.

Finally, let's talk about finding doctors or practitioners who are open to including spiritual stuff. This can be tricky, as not all doctors are comfy talking about spiritual things. Start by being up-front about what you want. When looking for a new doctor, ask if they're okay with talking about how your faith might play a role in your treatment.

Look for doctors who do "whole person" care. These folks often have a more complete view of health and might be more open to including spiritual elements. You might also look for faith-based health centers if they're in your area.

You are more than the sum of your parts! Your health is more than just treating symptoms. Remember, it's okay to shop around. If a doctor isn't open to talking about your spiritual needs, it's fine to look for someone who is. Your health journey is personal, and you deserve a doctor who respects all parts of who you are.

In the end, embracing this new way of thinking—one that mixes faith and science in healing—is a journey. It takes curiosity, openness and a willingness to look at health in a new way. But the rewards can be huge. By thinking about all parts of you—body, mind, emotions and spirit—you open the door to a deeper, more complete approach to health and healing. So take that first step. Start learning, start questioning and start exploring. Your whole self will thank you.

As you try these new ideas, be patient with yourself. Change takes time. It's normal to have ups and downs. Keep a diary to track how you're doing. Write down how you feel in your body and your mind. Celebrate small wins along the way. Maybe you spoke up at the doctor's office, or you found a new treatment that helps. These are all wins.

We are putting together a resource that organizes all of these ideas for those who don't have a holistic and integrated health community, called Connected Health. It combines the best of what I've learned over the last 25 years in one place where you learn about yourself and get questions answered. It combines many of the points and suggestions I make in this book into one centralized, easy-to-access resource. More on this later.

My patient Sarah didn't stop at trying new treatments. She kept learning and talking to people. She eventually got in to see me in person, adjusted her thyroid medicine, worked on mold toxin detox, started a low dose of naltrexone and with the right support, created the conditions her body needed to heal.

And just like Anna, Sarah didn't settle for what she was told. Led by her intuition and faith, she believed in something bigger—her ability to heal, the power of new possibilities and the idea that *health* was her natural state.

Let me tell you about another patient of mine, Jack—who also happens to be my father-in-law. In his late 20s, his health started to decline. Routine blood work showed a slight elevation in his liver enzymes, but his doctors dismissed it as insignificant. By his mid-30s, however, he was diagnosed with severe, life-threatening cirrhosis. At the time—38 years ago—doctors had no clear understanding of why this was happening. The only thing they knew for certain was that without a liver transplant, Jack wouldn't survive.

He was sent to the best transplant center in the country at the time—the University of Pittsburgh—where he received a liver transplant and was placed on a groundbreaking immunosuppressant medication called cyclosporine. That medication, which he remains on to this day, was cutting-edge at the time. Conventional medicine quite literally saved his life.

Fast forward several decades to the pandemic. Jack started experiencing severe neck and arm pain, eventually leading doctors to recommend neck surgery. But at the same time, he began suffering from unexplained fevers that would come and go. Despite multiple appointments, his primary care doctor could not determine the cause of these fevers, and his spine surgeon didn't see them as connected or as a concern.

Through family conversations, I learned about his mysterious symptoms, and I knew I had to step in. I ordered a basic panel of lab tests for fever of unknown origin. The results were undeniable—Jack had a glaring case of Lyme disease.

How did his primary care doctor miss this? A man living in Northern Virginia—one of the most Lyme-endemic areas in the country—went undiagnosed. I immediately started him on a six-week course of pulsed antibiotics, which brought the infection under control. He was then able to undergo neck surgery without complications.

But we didn't stop there. Over time it became clear that Jack's original liver disease was autoimmune in origin—it also looked like it was coming back, and he and his liver specialist were concerned. Understanding the delicate balance of his health, we incorporated additional liver support, including TUDCA—an ox bile extract known for breaking down biofilms and supporting liver function. Later, he transitioned to Ursodiol, the prescription version of

TUDCA, along with other targeted nutrients. And the result? His liver enzymes are the best they have been in over 30 years.

My wife often says that conventional medicine saved her father's life, but integrative and functional medicine allowed him to thrive. Thirty-eight years after receiving a liver transplant, Jack and my mother-in-law are still enjoying their retirement—going on bike trips, staying active and living life to the fullest.

This is the power of combining all forms of medicine—traditional, functional and integrative—without limiting beliefs. The combination of integrating your faith with all forms of medicine is the true path to total wellness. It's not about choosing one approach over another; it's about using everything available in a methodical, scientific and faith-driven way. The kind of faith that believes the body was designed to heal and repair itself when given the right support.

Jack's story is proof that when we remove barriers, think beyond conventional limits and trust in both science and the body's innate ability to heal, extraordinary things can happen.

Anna's healing journey flipped our understanding of medicine, faith and healing itself. Along the way, we encountered others who were struggling within the healthcare system—people who felt stuck, unheard or even hopeless. My experience with Anna helped me see deeper into their situations, to understand the obstacles they faced and, in some cases, to help change their trajectories toward healing.

Rather than replacing the standard treatments I had learned in medical school, at my practice we expanded our toolkit to include solutions that conventional medical institutions hadn't yet incorporated. This integrative approach doesn't merely manage symptoms—it meticulously investigates to uncover their root causes. It examines the whole person: body, mind, and spirit, recognizing that these elements form an interconnected system where imbalance in one area inevitably affects the others By combining the best of conventional medicine's diagnostic precision with functional medicine's systems-based healing framework, we created a more complete pathway to wellness that transformed Anna's prognosis from hopeless to hopeful.

Our journey took us to some pretty surprising places. We drove all the way to Canada so Anna could access a brain stimulator called PONS, a breakthrough device that helped stimulate her brain in ways that traditional treatments couldn't. We also turned to hyperbaric oxygen therapy to give her brain the extra boost it needed to heal. Hyperbaric oxygen therapy (HBOT) is a medical treatment that involves breathing pure oxygen in a pressurized environment. This treatment has been shown to increase the amount of oxygen dissolved in the blood plasma, allowing for enhanced oxygen delivery throughout the body, especially any parts that are damaged. HBOT promotes healing, helps fight infection and reduces tissue damage.

Along the way, we discovered just how deeply food influences health and how our physical environment can silently sabotage recovery. That's when everything clicked, and we designed a precision, personalized healthcare plan tailored specifically for Anna—built around her unique needs, biology and story. And that is what this truly is—personalized precision medicine.

We found out that faith and science can actually work together. They're not enemies—they can be partners in helping people heal. We established a "Head-Heart-Hands" method of making medical choices. It's a cool approach that uses science, faith, intuition and action together (more on this later).

And then we did something really different. We became homesteaders. We realized that true health starts from the ground up... literally. Healthy soil helps people stay healthy. Getting rid of toxins can help the body heal itself. Real, whole food is one of the best medicines out there.

We went from worried, fretting parents to people who could help others heal. From doubting "alternative" medicine to creating a new way of thinking about health. It's honest, it's real and it might change how you think about your own health.

As a husband and father, I have witnessed how being a mom can leave women feeling completely depleted and like they'rerunning on empty. But I've also been witnessing something remarkable unfolding—not just in research labs or places of worship, but right in the everyday rhythms of life: in kitchens, in quiet moments and in the hearts of women like my wife Becky. I say this as a medical professional who almost exclusively treats women—it's just how my practice has evolved over time. Currently about 80 percent of my patients are women and there's a good reason for that: Women are often the health leaders of their families. They're the first ones to notice when something's off, the first to dig for answers and the ones most willing to advocate fiercely for their loved ones. But in doing so, they often sacrifice their own well-being. And in the midst of that sacrifice, these women—exhausted, overlooked and often running on empty— are becoming ground zero for a quiet revolution. It's the extraordinary intersection of faith and science—and it's transforming lives in ways we never thought possible.

This transformation wasn't just happening in my clinic or in academic journals. It was happening right next to me. Because while we were fighting for Anna's healing, another story was unfolding in our own home—one I didn't fully understand until much later.

While I was diving into research, learning functional medicine and fighting the system for Anna's future, my wife Becky was fighting her own battle with chronic illness. Her journey would ultimately shape not just our family's approach to health, but the very foundation of our practice. What I didn't fully grasp then was that Becky's instincts about health—the same instincts that led us to Anna, pushed us toward real food and challenged conventional medical wisdom—came from her own body's hard-won wisdom. She had been navigating chemical sensitivities and systemic dysfunction long before we had names for these conditions.

Let me turn this over to Becky to share her story in her own words, because this is a crucial puzzle piece for the big picture of how faith and science truly intersect in the messy, painful and beautiful reality of healing.

Becky's Health Journey

In a family, nothing happens in a vacuum. Let me share something most people don't know about our family's journey. While Aaron was learning to help Anna and his patients, I was fighting my own battle—one that nearly broke me but ultimately shaped everything about how we approach health today as a family.

It started subtly. In grad school, I developed crippling anxiety out of nowhere. The brain fog was so thick I could barely keep up with my coursework. I almost dropped out multiple times—my roommate Jennifer's encouragement and support were the only reasons I stayed. Something had shifted in my body, and I didn't know what or why. I'd always connected faith to health—I had more sensibility about healing than most—but I was struggling to understand what was happening. This wasn't cancer or liver disease like my dad had. I didn't yet know about detox pathways or chemical sensitivities. I prayed for relief and wisdom, but the dots weren't connecting. Sometimes faith means trusting there are answers even when you can't see the full picture yet. And that means waiting patiently.

Fifteen years later, Aaron and I finally connected the dots. I was visiting my parents, who had just installed new carpet throughout their house. By the end of the visit, I was exhausted, not able to sleep and feeling completely off. I remembered that the same thing happened once at a hotel with fresh renovations. That's when the lightbulb went off—formaldehyde. I'd spent months in an anatomy lab during grad school, surrounded by formaldehyde fumes. That exposure had triggered something in my body that never fully resolved.

But the real crash came later. I was juggling so much—Anna's intensive needs and three adoptions, each with their own complexities (including one that involved years of heartbreaking uncertainty and legal battles). The stress was crushing. During this time, I'd gained weight and made a desperate decision that nearly destroyed me.

I started a program that promised quick weight loss that required extreme calorie restriction for six weeks. It turned out to be the perfect storm for my body—rapid fat loss released stored toxins, and I didn't get enough protein to help my body process them. My underlying issues with chemical sensitivity and hypermobility (that we didn't yet understand) exacerbated the issue.

The result? Five years of debilitating chronic fatigue.

The timing couldn't have been worse. While I was barely functioning health-wise, life kept throwing curveballs. I walked through devastating loss with someone I loved dearly—the kind of tragedy that shakes you to your core. I discovered multiple uterine fibroids that would eventually require a hysterectomy. (Sidebar: Women, make your own health a priority alongside everyone else's!) Layer upon layer of emotional stress, grief and new, confusing physical challenges—all while my body was already in crisis.

I would try to exercise—doing 30 seconds of high-intensity intervals—and immediately need to sleep. I wasn't just tired, but going through body-crashing, can't-function exhaustion. There were days I couldn't get out of bed, but I had to because my kids needed me to be their arms and legs. Aaron had to come home from work and make dinner because I struggled to keep standing long enough to cook. I missed so much of our kids' lives during those years.

During those dark years, prayer became my lifeline. Some days, when getting out of bed felt impossible, all I could do was whisper, "God, help me through this day." I always got up. My family needed me. My faith wasn't just comforting—it was survival. It gave me a reason to keep fighting when my body wanted to quit. "Hartmans do hard things" became our family mantra. I'd repeat it while forcing myself to get up, to care for our kids, to show up even when every cell in my body screamed for rest.

The worst part wasn't the physical exhaustion—it was the fear. Every setback triggered a panic that I was crashing again, that I'd lose another five years. On a family trip, I tried to walk up a steep hill. Halfway up, I felt that familiar exhaustion creeping in. My body started screaming that I was near death. I fled down that hill, convinced I was about to crash for another five years.

I'd also dealt with toxic shock syndrome—mysterious monthly fevers, aches and pains that no one could explain. After over a year of suffering through these cycles, I finally connected the dots myself. Even Aaron with all his medical training hadn't recognized it. It was another reminder that sometimes we have to be our own detectives, trusting what our bodies are telling us even when the experts can't see it.

Then our son's accident added trauma on top of everything. He was crushed in an elevator—it was a miracle that he survived. But for years after, every time he disappeared on our farm for even a few minutes, I'd panic. My body would go into complete sympathetic overdrive. Even when he'd reappear perfectly fine, it would take me four or five hours to calm down and regulate. I lived in constant fear that everyone I loved would die in some catastrophic way. Through it all, I kept praying—for safety, for healing from this consuming terror, for the strength to navigate each day without being paralyzed by fear.

The turning point for my chronic fatigue came when I decided to try the same approaches that Aaron was learning about for Anna, like the PEMF device he'd been using with patients. When I finally tried it, it was like a light switched on. That simple tool cracked open the door that had been closed for five painful years. The fog began to lift. For the first time in years, I had enough energy to start making the small changes I knew I needed.

Years later, at a Swiss detox clinic, I discovered I needed much more protein than average to support detoxification. They tried to put me on a raw vegan diet, and I went completely toxic—my body crashed hard. It wasn't until they gave me amino acids and let me eat eggs that I stabilized. My labs confirmed it—my white blood cell count went up to over 20 and inflammatory markers were through the roof until we added protein back.

But even as my physical health improved, I was still carrying trauma—not just from our son's elevator accident, but from years of medical crisis, uncertainty and pushing through when my body was screaming for rest. I'd been praying for years for release from this trauma. When a breathwork opportunity came up, I felt drawn to try it. I was skeptical because it seemed a little too "out there"—but faith had taught me that healing can come through unexpected channels. In one intensive session with Sachin Patel's holotropic breathwork (no drugs, just breathing techniques), something shifted. That constant foreboding, that panic about losing everyone I loved—it stopped. Not gradually—immediately. It has never come back.

Here's what I've learned through all of this: Healing isn't linear. You don't just get better in a straight line. You have ups and downs, setbacks and breakthroughs. But each challenge teaches you something. Each tool you gain comes with you to the next battle.

I understand now why I pushed Aaron toward functional medicine, why I insisted on real food for our kids, why I fought against fluoride and unnecessary medications. My body has taught me, through brutal experience, that we're more sensitive and complex than conventional medicine acknowledges. That trauma lives in our bodies, not just our minds. That sometimes the "treatment" can be worse than the condition.

But more than that, this journey taught me that faith and science aren't opposites—they're dance partners. Faith gave me the courage to question the status quo, to trust my body's wisdom when doctors dismissed my concerns, to keep searching when answers seemed impossible. Science gave us the tools, but faith gave us the why—the unshakeable belief that we were made for health, that healing was possible even when everything seemed hopeless. Every morning, I'd pray for wisdom, for strength and for answers. And slowly, through both divine guidance and scientific discovery, those prayers were answered.

This journey also prepared me to help build our practice in ways I never expected. Because I've lived the patient experience—the dismissal, the wrong treatments and the slow journey to answers—I understand what people need when they walk through our doors. I've shaped every aspect of how we serve patients because I know what it's like to be desperate for someone to truly listen and help.

The truth is, I'm still on this journey. I'm more careful now, more aware of my body's signals. When something feels off, I don't push through—I listen. I've learned that being strong doesn't mean ignoring your limits; it means knowing them and working wisely within them while constantly expanding what's possible.

Aaron often says, "You were made for health." I believe that. But I also know that for some of us, finding that health requires walking through the darkness first. The question is: What will you do with what the journey teaches you?

The journey taught me everything, and now, I can't un-know what I know. I can't unsee what I've seen. Seeing the dramatic shifts in myself and the miracles in my kids' health changed me. It changed how I show up in the world, and finding your optimal health will change you too.

Learning From Each Other

Becky's journey fundamentally changed how I practice medicine. Here was someone I loved, someone I watched suffer despite all my medical training, teaching me lessons no textbook ever could. Her experience with chemical sensitivities preceded my understanding of environmental medicine by over a decade. Her need for higher protein during detox revealed principles I now use with every patient. Her trauma response after our son's accident opened my eyes to how deeply the nervous system impacts every aspect of health.

But perhaps most importantly, Becky showed me that the patient often knows their body better than any expert. When she pushed back against fluoride, she was right. When she insisted on real food over medical formulas, she was right. When she recognized that her crashes weren't just "stress" but serious systemic dysfunction, she was right. The best way for me to honor and respect my wife was to extend that same trust and respect to my patients.

This is the miracle of faith-driven science—not that faith replaces science, but that sometimes faith keeps us searching when science hasn't caught up yet. Becky's faith in her body's ability to heal, even when I didn't fully understand what was happening, pushed both of us toward answers that conventional medicine wasn't providing.

Together, our journey—both with Anna and with Becky's health
—created something neither of us could have built alone. It's why our
practice looks different, why we listen differently, why we never
dismiss a patient who says "something's not right" even when their
labs look normal: because we've lived it. We know that healing
happens in the intersection of rigorous science and unwavering faith
—faith in the body's wisdom, faith in the journey and faith that
answers exist even when they're not yet visible. Faith and medicine
are intertwined, and we have committed our practice to fostering
their growth and thereby helping our patients flourish.

The ripple effects of what we learned continue to spread. When
you've walked through your own health crisis and come out the other
side, you can't help but see medicine differently. Every patient who
walks through our doors benefits from lessons learned in the hardest
moments—when conventional approaches failed us, when we had to
forge our own path, when faith kept us searching for answers that
science hadn't yet provided.

This journey has naturally evolved into something we never
anticipated—a highly selective approach to care that mirrors the
intensive, investigative work that transformed Anna's trajectory. For
the rare individual facing complex, multi-system challenges that
conventional medicine has abandoned, or for those seeking to optimize performance at the highest levels, we've developed what we call
Personalized Precision Medicine.

Personalized Precision Medicine is not for everyone—in fact, it's
appropriate for less than one in a thousand people we encounter. It's
ideal for those battling a condition others have declared "uncurable"
or for executives, athletes or high performers whose bodies and
minds are professional assets. This practice represents the pinnacle
of everything we've learned about personalized optimization. It's the
kind of medicine practiced when time constraints disappear, when
every biochemical pathway can be explored and when no stone
remains unturned in the pursuit of answers—or peak performance.
We don't advertise this work broadly—the right individuals, whether

seeking healing or optimization, tend to find their way to us when they're ready for this level of commitment to their transformation.

What matters most is this: You were made for health. Your body has the ability to self-heal and self-repair. If you can just find what is blocking your body's natural healing and replace what is lacking, your body will do what it was made to do. I know this to be true because I've seen it in my family and in thousands of patients as well.

So to every exhausted mom out there, hear me loud and clear—your faith holds power. It's the foundation for transformation. It's your reason for never giving up. And when you align your faith with real, science-backed strategies, you unlock a whole new level of health, energy and purpose. Faith gives you the why. Science fills in the how. Together, they change everything.

As you keep going on your own health journey, remember that you know yourself best. Trust your feelings, ask questions and keep learning. Your body can do amazing things to heal. By using all parts of yourself—body, mind and spirit—you're giving yourself the best chance to be healthy. Your path to feeling better starts now. Trust yourself, stay curious and keep going. Your whole self will thank you. Now that you're ready to elevate your health, let's outline some clear steps you can take to empower yourself and excel as an informed advocate. Keep reading for a how-to.

Scan the QR code below with your phone's camera. This will direct you to open a web page that provides instant access to our comprehensive collection of free resources.

12

SEVEN STEPS TO JUMP-START SUCCESS

As you've read in all the previous chapters, many of my patients have experiences like Anna's, and they all prove one thing: You must be the hero of your own journey. No one is coming to rescue you. You need to step forward, claim your quest and build your Fellowship of the Ring. But you don't have to fight alone—you need to build your own superstar team. In this chapter I'm going to give you tangible, action-oriented suggestions for tracking your health, your challenges and your triumphs—a step-by-step guide to owning your own health, wellness and recovery journey.

That means you're going to have homework, like tracking your symptoms, creating a map to guide your way, assembling the right allies—doctors who listen, friends who support, coaches who help you along the way and family who advocate for you. But the most important action item is to never give up, even when the road gets tough.

Keep a Health Journal: Your Own Map

Like Frodo marking every step toward Mordor in *The Lord of the*

Rings, you need to track your journey. So let's get practical with one of the most transformative tools in functional medicine's approach: comprehensive health journaling. This isn't just another item on your to-do list—it's the foundation upon which personalized healing is built. Create a dedicated space, whether digital or paper-based, to methodically track multiple dimensions of your health: your energy levels throughout the day, physical symptoms as they emerge and subside, emotional states, sleep quality, digestive function and detailed food intake. Include everything—not just meals, but snacks, beverages, timing of consumption and your physical and emotional responses afterward.

This practice illuminates connections that would otherwise remain invisible—like the headache that consistently appears 48 hours after consuming certain foods or the energy crash that follows exposure to specific environments. Where conventional medicine might see random, disconnected symptoms, your journal reveals the underlying patterns. I've witnessed patients make break-through discoveries after years of diagnostic dead ends simply by recognizing these patterns. One woman discovered her debilitating migraines correlated not with any particular food, but with specific combinations of foods eaten within the same meal. It just happened to be at her favorite weekly Mongolian restaurant. Another realized her joint pain intensified precisely two days after consuming dairy—a delay that had concealed the connection for decades.

Keep a daily health diary, noting:

- Energy levels (scale of one to five, with one being very low energy and five feeling ready for the day)
- Mood (scale of one to five, with one being unmotivated and depressed-feeling, and five feeling optimistic about your day and life)
- Pain or symptoms (scale of one to five, with one being low and manageable pain, and five feeling extremely unable to function)

A sample entry might look like this:

- *June 15th: Energy - 3/5, Mood - 2/5, Dizziness - 2/5.*
- *Slept seven hours, ate salad for lunch, and a 30-minute walk in the evening.*
- *Felt less dizzy today after drinking more water. A storm front came in and it rained all day. Slept poorly the night prior.*

When you rate your energy, mood and pain or symptom levels on that scale, over time, you will observe clear patterns—clues to help you understand what helps and what worsens your symptoms.

With Lizzy, once I had the diagnosis, we began our strategic plan. Yes, she needed to shift her diet, get more consistent sleep and commit to regular movement. But with POTS patients, even small foundational changes—like boosting electrolytes and fluids, wearing compression stockings and doing targeted physical exercises—can create immediate shifts in blood pressure and brain blood flow. I also added in a low dose of naltrexone as current research shows its ability to lower the brain inflammation associated with POTS ("Low-Dose Naltrexone's Utility for Non-Cancer Centralized Pain Conditions," Rupp et al., 2023; "Low-Dose Naltrexone and Traumatic Brain Injury," Dickson, n.d.; "The Use of Low-Dose Naltrexone as a Novel Anti-Inflammatory Treatment for Chronic Pain," Younger et al., 2014). Lizzy soon noticed a dramatic drop in anxiety, just from these simple adjustments. Then came the hardest part: retraining the brain to help her autonomic nervous system recalibrate and find balance again.

A side note and golden nugget for you: Low-dose naltrexone is now becoming more mainstream. It's an inexpensive way to balance your immune system, lower inflammation and improve gut function. Research shows it can help with long COVID, autoimmune diseases, weight loss, post-concussive syndrome, chronic fatigue syndrome/ME, SIBO, autism and more ("Low-Dose Naltrexone [LDN]: Review of Therapeutic Utilization," Toljan and Vrooman, 2018). It sounds too good to be true, but it's not. It's been around since 1984 (over 40 years) and it's super safe. If you want to take a deep dive into this new cutting-edge therapy as well as get a copy of *UnCurable Health Journal*, scan the QR code at the end of this chapter. We also have a sample journal to get you started.

Conduct a Thorough Environmental Audit

In addition to your health journal, expand your investigation to your environment. This is an even more comprehensive health audit, and it is crucial. Your surroundings directly impact your biochemistry in ways that most conventional practitioners never consider. Systematically assess the chemicals present in your daily life—from cleaning products and personal care items to furniture treatments and yard maintenance products. Evaluate your water quality through proper testing, not just assuming municipal water is safe. Consider air quality both inside and outside your home, including potential mold exposure, off-gassing from new materials and ventilation effectiveness.

Take a walk around your home. What do you see in your kitchen? Is it stocked with nourishing foods or filled with temptations? Small changes—like placing a bowl of fruit on the counter instead of a bag of chips—can make a big difference in your daily choices.

Now, step into your bedroom. This is where your body *heals*. Is it a restful space? Do you have a consistent bedtime, or do screens and stress keep you up? Sleep is *critical*—without quality rest, your body can't repair itself, your energy, mood and even cravings can spiral out of control, and we often don't even know why.

If sleep is a struggle, apply the tiny habit method. Instead of forcing yourself into an elaborate bedtime routine, start small. Dim the lights 30 minutes before bed. Put your phone across the room. Take ten deep breaths before lying down. Small wins lead to big results. For more suggestions, visit our wellness platform at Connected Health where we have an entire section devoted just to sleep. That's how important it is!

These environmental factors aren't secondary considerations—they're often the hidden triggers that keep chronic conditions active despite your best efforts with diet and supplements. With my wife, Becky, we discovered how seemingly innocuous environmental exposures were undermining her progress, creating inflammatory cascades that no medication could resolve. She has a specific sensitivity to formaldehyde found in new carpets and especially in new hotels.

To simplify this process, I've created several resources. After carefully reviewing the Harvard School of Public Health's comprehensive *Healthy Home Guide*, I've distilled its essential wisdom into a series of accessible video shorts available by accessing the QR code at the end of this chapter. This resource can literally transform your living space from a source of ongoing toxic exposure into a healing sanctuary that supports recovery at the cellular level. Even small adjustments—like removing shoes at the door or switching to glass food storage containers—can significantly reduce your body's toxic burden. I've created a *Foundations of Functional Medicine* quick guide as well. This reviews the health foundations required for any self-healing program.

Remember, in functional medicine, we recognize that your health story is written not just by what you consume, but by everything you contact. Becoming fluent in reading these influences is often the missing link in resolving persistent health challenges.

Seek Ways to De-Stress

Pause and ask yourself—how stressed are you *really*? Stress affects everything: your cravings, your digestion and your sleep. If you're constantly in fight-or-flight mode, your body holds onto weight, your mind feels foggy and your energy crashes.

Identify a single moment in your day where stress builds up— maybe it's before a meeting, during your commute or when you get home after a long day. Now, create a tiny habit to interrupt that stress cycle. It could be three deep breaths, stretching your arms overhead or stepping outside for fresh air. Small moments of calm add up.

Don't forget about your mind and emotions. Stress, worry and feeling down can all mess with your physical health. Try adding stress-busters like meditation or tai chi to your day. Even just taking a walk or a few deep breaths when you're stressed can help. Navy SEALs use box breathing to keep their nervous system in check when they are in combat! Herbs like ashwagandha and nutrients like L-theanine both help lower cortisol and have a calming effect. This stuff actually works!

Box Breathing

Box breathing, also known as square breathing or four-square breathing, is a simple yet powerful technique used to calm the nervous system, reduce stress and enhance focus. It is a form of deep, rhythmic breathwork that gets its name from the four equal steps involved in the process, which mimic the sides of a box.

This technique is widely used by high-stress professionals like military personnel, police officers and first responders, who refer to it as "tactical breathing," to maintain composure and performance under pressure.

It works by activating the parasympathetic nervous system, often referred to as the "rest and digest" system. When stressed, the body typically engages the sympathetic nervous system, leading to the "fight or flight" response, characterized by increased heart rate, shallow breathing and elevated stress hormones (like cortisol).

By intentionally slowing and regulating the breath, box breathing sends a signal to the brain that the body is safe, counteracting the stress response. This controlled breathing pattern helps lower heart rate, regulate blood pressure and promotes a state of relaxation and clarity.

The box breathing technique involves four equal steps, typically counted to four:

1. **Exhale (count of four):** Gently and completely exhale all the air from your lungs.

2. **Hold (count of four):** Hold your breath with empty lungs for a count of four.
3. **Inhale (count of four):** Slowly inhale through your nose, filling your lungs completely, for a count of four.
4. **Hold (count of four):** Hold your breath with full lungs for a count of four.

The cycle is then repeated. Many practitioners find it helpful to visualize tracing the sides of a square as they perform each step. With regular practice, you might notice reduced stress and anxiety, emotional regulation, physiological regulation, better sleep and improved focus.

Celebrate Small Wins: Your Personal Victory Jar

Every battle won matters. Maybe you walked 10 minutes without feeling exhausted. Maybe you had a full day without a headache. Write these victories down. Also write down what was going on the days or weeks prior and the day of.

Consider a "victory jar." Write down every milestone—no matter how small—and fold it up and put it in the jar. On hard days, pull them out and remind yourself how far you've come.

Find a Healing Partner

Now, let's talk about finding good integrative practitioners. This isn't as easy as picking a name out of a hat. You want someone who gets this new way of thinking. The right doctor is not just a healer—they're a guide, leading you through the unknown, a teacher explaining the why along the way. The root word in Latin for doctor is *docēre*, which means "to teach." Teaching at its core is what a good doctor will do.

Start by asking friends or family who've had luck with integrative medicine. If that's a bust, or more commonly you just don't know anyone, try online directories like the Institute for Functional Medicine's (IFM) search tool. We have a resource for this through Connected Health as well. It's our answer to those wanting to apply this kind of thinking to their health and their families' health, from the comfort of their own home, with me as their guide.

If you want to see someone in person, start by using the Institute for Functional Medicine's website and the American Academy of Anti-Aging and Regenerative Medicine. Ideally you'd find someone certified through both organizations. Their training is not the same but 100 percent complementary, and I've done them both. Once you have a few names, it's time to dig deeper. Do your homework—check out their personal or clinic websites, read any reviews and look for articles they've written. You want to get a sense of how they think and practice. Functional providers who are truly committed to helping others often share their knowledge through blogs, podcasts and interviews. Explore these materials to learn how they approach care. This is more than just choosing a name from a list—this is your health we're talking about. It's an investment in your future, so don't take it lightly. Look for practitioners who emphasize treating the whole person and prioritize identifying root causes instead of just managing symptoms. And if you're located near us in Virginia or willing to travel to see us, we welcome you to our practice—where you'll join a dedicated team committed to supporting your health journey, each member bringing unique expertise to overcome the obstacles in your path.

When you're ready to book, don't be shy about asking questions. A good integrative doctor will love your curiosity. Ask about their training, their story, how they treat people and how they mix different methods. Inquire if they include things like food, stress management and lifestyle changes in their plans. Ask about some of the advanced therapies and topics you are learning about in this book or have read about elsewhere. If you don't know what questions to ask, we have a Q&A section on our website that consists of the top questions people have asked us over the years (**AaronHartman-MD.com**). Use that as a guide during your journey. For our practice, we have already answered all these questions and more on our website. So if you're not sure where to start or even what to look for, feel free to use that for a jumping-off point.

During your first visit, watch how the doctor treats you. Notice if they really listen to your health story. Observe if they ask about your life, your stress, your sleep. These are good signs they're taking a truly integrative approach. How long is the visit? Your first visit should be at least an hour. I typically take two and a half hours, but most intakes are not that long. Anything less than an hour just isn't enough time.

Maybe you like the doctor you are currently working with and they are open to helping you, but they aren't functionally trained. We have a resource, "How to Talk to Your Doctor," that helps guide you on how to use resources you already have (your current doctor) and combine it with information you are learning here, on our website, from an online platform or from your own personal research. (The QR code for this resource is at the end of this chapter.)

For those who can't find a practitioner close to them, we have an answer for that as well. We have created an online resource called Connected Health—a platform that supports individuals and families applying this type of thinking from home. Some of the free resources we are sharing in the book are part of the resources we have created for Connected Health.

Remember, this is a team effort. You're not just sitting back and taking orders—you're part of your health journey. Be ready to put in some work. Your doctor or whomever you are working with might suggest changing your diet, taking supplements or tweaking your lifestyle. They might want different tests than you're used to. Be open to these ideas, but don't be afraid to ask if something doesn't make sense.

If you are working with someone you know, like and trust already, there is no need to go looking for someone else. But you need to respect the limitations placed on them by our current healthcare system. Our resource, "How to Talk to your Doctor," will guide you through how to work with them within the system to get you on the path to healing.

Build Your Fellowship—The Team That Carries You

Healing is not a solo quest. Frodo needed Sam, Legolas, Aragorn —the entire Fellowship. You need:

- Supportive family and friends
- Online educational resources
- Healing routines—meal prepping, stress management, movement
- The right practitioners along the way

Most of all, you need relentless determination.

Share Your Story: Be Someone's Light in the Darkness

Anna's story helped me change Lizzy's life. And now, Lizzy's story will help others.

Your story could do the same. Even if you're still in the middle of your journey, share it. Start a blog, post on social media or speak at local events. Someone out there needs to hear that they are not alone. This is your journey—own it.

Every great quest comes with challenges. There will be good days and bad. But if you keep moving forward—tracking your progress, celebrating small victories and never giving up—you will find your way. Your health quest is uniquely yours. What works for one person may not work for another, but the goal remains the same: true healing.

So trust the process. Keep going. Never stop searching for answers.

Like Frodo standing at the edge of Mount Doom, you have a choice. Will you let the weight of your symptoms drag you down? Or will you take control and claim your victory?

Here's what I've learned after watching thousands of patients transform their health: The people who achieve the most profound healing are often those who turn their pain into purpose. Anna's struggle didn't just change her life—it informed my entire approach to medicine and has now impacted tens of thousands of patients. My wife Becky's journey through chronic fatigue and chemical sensitivities didn't just teach us about detoxification and trauma—it shaped how we serve every person who walks through our doors feeling dismissed and desperate. This is the pattern throughout history: The greatest champions of change are those who've walked through the fire themselves.

Nelson Mandela's 27 years in prison didn't break him—it forged him into a leader who could heal a nation. Martin Luther King Jr.'s suffering under systemic racism didn't silence him—it gave him the moral authority to awaken a country's conscience. Your health crisis, your struggle, your darkest moments aren't just obstacles to overcome—they're your credentials for helping others. When you transform your health against all odds, you don't just heal yourself; you become living proof that transformation is possible. You become the beacon of hope that someone else desperately needs to see.

Every choice you make toward healing, every story you share, every friend or family member you inspire creates a ripple effect that can literally change the world. I've done the math: It would only take a few thousand people—people like you who refuse to accept "uncurable" as final—actively sharing their transformation stories to fundamentally shift our entire healthcare system. The question isn't whether your struggle can have meaning and impact. The question is: *What will you do with the wisdom your pain has given you?* You have probably felt the isolation of navigating the system, a diagnosis, treatment and finding the right care. I'm writing this book in hopes of helping you feel less alone. You are a unique and miraculous being, and your health is a reflection of how you feel about yourself. While your diagnosis or treatment may make you feel like the exception to the rules, it really just points out that you are exceptional. Keep reading to learn about how you can transform your thinking and become a powerful player in the change we are creating together.

Scan the QR code below with your phone's camera. This will direct you to open a web page that provides instant access to our comprehensive collection of free resources.

13

YOU ARE EXCEPTIONAL

Anna's progress is still mind-blowing to this day. As of this year, she is able to swim in a pool without a life jacket or preserver for 30 minutes, then get out of the pool all by herself. Unassisted! (Of course I'm there the entire time as a spotter.) These results totally flip conventional wisdom on its head (but maybe by now you have come to expect it). Here's the deal: When we really dig into root causes and treat the whole person, we can do what seems impossible. Anna's case proved that chronic conditions aren't always a life sentence. By mixing the best of old-school and new-school methods, we saw results that left even the most skeptical doctors scratching their heads.

But this isn't just about Anna, Jack, Lizzy, Abby or Khalil. Like my daughter, all of my patients are exceptional—and so are you. If there are rules in medicine, it's absolutely acceptable for you to consider yourself the exception to those rules. And that means that your recovery and health can *also* be exceptional. I get the skepticism— really, I do. But here's what I've seen with my own eyes: over a thousand people experiencing what once seemed like impossible changes. Not because they believed in magic, but because they dared to look at things differently—and had the faith to take small, science-backed steps that added up to big results.

Are you starting to see the point? Maybe you, or your loved ones or your friends or family can hold onto enough faith and hope to see those same kinds of changes. This isn't about wishful thinking. It's about real outcomes, driven by a deeper understanding of what's truly going on in the body and mind.

Skepticism isn't the enemy—apathy is. So question everything. Test it. Kick the tires, so to speak. But don't close the door before you've even looked through the window. Because the people I've worked with didn't just hope—they acted. They are exceptional because of all their hard work and willingness to take charge and challenge a system resistant to change. And that's where transformation begins.

So if this feels unfamiliar—or even a bit fantastic—remember: The greatest power often hides in plain sight. This is a hero's journey —Anna is my hero, and you are too. Like Lucy stepping through the wardrobe or Frodo setting off with an ordinary ring. In those stories, ancient truths were rediscovered, and ordinary people became part of something extraordinary. That's what this kind of "deep medicine" feels like. Not magic—but something just as rare in our rushed, surface-level world: healing that touches every layer of who you are.

The journey might not look like anything you expected. But if you're willing to take the first step, you might just find a world more real—and more powerful—than anything you've known before. You are exceptional. Be the hero of your own story.

It's smart to be cautious. There's a ton of nonsense out there. But here's the thing: This approach isn't about ditching science. It's about taking it to the next level—and the evidence speaks for itself. We're talking about hard facts, serious studies and real results. Functional medicine isn't some fringe idea anymore. Institutions like the Cleveland Clinic (which now runs the largest functional medicine clinic in the US) are leading the way. And it doesn't stop there. Brigham and Women's Hospital and Harvard Medical School's Osher Center for Integrative Medicine offer consultations that combine functional medicine with acupuncture, yoga and nutritional health coaching. George Washington University even offers a Master's in Health Sciences in Integrative Medicine with a strictly evidence-based approach. The University of South Florida has a certification in Personalized Medicine, and the University of Arizona's Andrew Weil Center for Integrative Medicine trains fellows in holistic care.

See? We're not replacing regular medicine—we're supercharging it. More and more long-term studies show these methods work ("Association of the Functional Medicine Model of Care with Patient-Reported Health-Related Quality-of-Life Outcomes," Beidelschies et al., 2019). Why? Because we're tackling the root of the problem, not just slapping Band-Aids on symptoms. The future of medicine is already here—it's just that no one's paying to advertise it.

Let's be real—changing your lifestyle isn't easy. But you're not going it alone. We've got your back with solid support. It's like learning to ride a bike. You start wobbly, but before you know it, you're cruising. Remember to take baby steps—small changes add up to big results. And once you start feeling better, you'll wonder how you ever lived any other way.

This isn't some woo-woo nonsense. We're deep into cutting-edge science. We're talking genetics, systems biology, peptides, metabolic medicine and a deep dive into how your environment and lifestyle shape your health. Targeting the root cause of disease and illness—this is as scientific as it gets. And the evidence keeps piling up. Every day, more studies back up what we're seeing in practice ("Patient Outcomes and Costs Associated with Functional Medicine-Based Care in a Shared Versus Individual Setting for Patients with Chronic Conditions," Beidelschies et al, 2021). We're not running from science; we're running toward it, arms wide open.

I get it. Trying something new can be scary. But here's the deal: This isn't about throwing out everything you know. We're not ditching regular medicine—we're making it better. Remember, I started as a traditional doctor—I'm a professor at the local medical school. I've published in *Lancet* and I've run a clinical research company. But I also know when to use alternative methods and when old-school approaches are best. Our goal? To give you the safest, most effective care possible. It's not either/or—it's both/and. We're giving you more options, not fewer. This is true personalized precision medicine.

Think of your health like a three-legged stool: body, mind and spirit. Ignore any leg, and the entire structure collapses. This approach recognizes that you're not just a collection of symptoms—you're a whole person with an integrated system. While we address physical issues, we simultaneously examine how emotions, beliefs and life experience influence your physiology.

For many patients, this leads us into what I call "trauma-informed medicine"—a field that examines how past experiences physically reshape your nervous system. The scientific literature terms this "trauma neurobiology," but the implications are profoundly practical (*The Body Keeps the Score*, van der Kolk, 2014). I've observed a consistent pattern: Patients often reach about 50 to 60 percent improvement and then mysteriously plateau. The missing piece? Unresolved trauma, undiagnosed PTSD or even the trauma of the illness itself rewiring neural pathways and disrupting the body's healing mechanisms.

This recognition demands an entirely different toolkit—one that conventional medical training simply doesn't provide. Your nervous system acts as the captain of your body's healing processes, and when it's locked in a trauma response, physiological recovery stalls regardless of perfect lab values or medication compliance. This explains why two patients with identical conditions and treatments can experience dramatically different outcomes.

Within Connected Health, we're developing a comprehensive platform specifically addressing this critical gap. This wasn't part of my practice five or 10 years ago, but today, trauma-informed approaches have become standard tools in my clinical arsenal. I didn't choose this direction—my patients' healing journeys demanded it. As with everything in my practice, I meet patients where they are and adapt to what their bodies truly need, not what medical textbooks prescribe.

Let me be crystal clear about something fundamental: This isn't about imposing any particular healing system, belief system or spiritual framework. It's about acknowledging an undeniable clinical reality I've witnessed thousands of times—the mind and belief system can either supercharge healing or become an insurmountable barrier that no medication can overcome.

For many patients locked in healing plateaus, breakthrough comes through unexpected channels. Some experience profound transformations through evidence-based trauma therapies like EMDR, which literally rewires neural pathways, or Internal Family Systems (IFS) therapy, which resolves inner conflicts that are blocking physiological healing. Others find their turning point through meditation practices that demonstrably alter inflammatory markers and hormone cascades. Still others experience remarkable recoveries through brain retraining protocols like Primal Trust, which reset and refine dysregulated nervous systems.

And yes—for many, spirituality provides a framework that makes everything else possible. I've watched patients for whom prayer becomes as physiologically powerful as prescription medication, creating measurable shifts in healing metrics that science can observe but not fully explain. And this point is key! **Science is a method for making discoveries, but it doesn't explain why they are happening the way they are.**

The key insight isn't which approach works best—it's understanding that healing often requires engaging the whole person. One of my roles is to honor the reality that the mind-body connection, often anchored by spiritual practice, creates healing pathways that purely physical interventions cannot open.

This is personalized medicine at its most profound. Whether you're deeply spiritual or completely secular, we meet you exactly where you are, providing tools that are tailored to your unique wiring. The goal is pure and simple—it's transformation. And the pathway there must be as individual as you are.

There is a reason why all clinical research in the US requires a placebo arm. It's because even sham treatments have positive results.

The question isn't *if* they work; it's if the therapy being studied works better than a nontherapeutic intervention. All standard of care therapies are based on this concept! So even the research system gets the power of the mind-body connection, though they won't say that out loud.

But it is also a balancing act, for sure. We're all about empowering you, not overwhelming you. Think of it like learning a new language. We start with the basics and build from there. We break down complex ideas into bite-sized pieces. And here's the key: constant communication. Feeling lost? Speak up. Need to slow down? Let us know. We'll adjust the pace to match your stride. You're the expert on you, and we're here to guide, not dictate.

Our understanding of environmental impacts has exploded. We're not just talking about obvious pollutants anymore; we're looking at the air you breathe, the water you drink, even the cookware you use ("Federal Court Rules Against EPA in Lawsuit Over Fluoride in Water," Tin, 2024). We've developed seriously sophisticated ways to spot how environmental factors are messing with your personal health. It's like being a health detective, uncovering hidden clues. This lets us create super-personalized plans to detox and modify your environment. It's a field that's always changing, and we're changing right along with it.

As I'm writing this, just this past month the FDA put a ban on red dye No. 3 due to its cancer risk ("FDA to Revoke Authorization for the Use of Red No. 3 in Food and Ingested Drugs," FDA.gov, 2025). This past fall a federal judge put an injunction on the EPA to address the risk of fluoride in the water lowering IQ. Red dye No. 3 was approved by the FDA in 1969 and fluoride has been in the water system since 1945. We can't just wait for the "experts" to get it right. We have to advocate for ourselves.

However, we cannot expect overnight miracles or try to overhaul our entire life in one go. This isn't about extreme makeovers—it's about sustainable changes. People often get bummed out if they don't wake up feeling like a superhero after a week. We really drive home the importance of patience and sticking with it. And here's a crucial point: What works for your buddy might not work for you. That's why personalization is key. Your health journey is as unique as your fingerprint.

We're like scientific tightrope walkers, balancing skepticism and open-mindedness. We've got one foot firmly planted in rigorous research, constantly reviewing studies. But we've also got an ear to the ground for new ideas and ancient wisdom that might not have hit the mainstream yet. We apply the scientific method to everything—even stuff that seems out there at first glance. We're after real, measurable outcomes. It's about being curious enough to explore, but critical enough to question. In the end, if it works and we can prove it, we're all in—no matter how unconventional it might seem.

So here's the bottom line: Things have to change. Doing the same thing over and over while expecting a different result isn't just wishful thinking—it's insanity. We've reached the point where business as usual is failing far too many people. It's not enough to patch symptoms and call it progress. It's time to demand more, to expect better and to act boldly. You are exceptional and you deserve a system that treats you that way—one that evolves with science, that honors your individuality and that refuses to settle for "good enough." The future of healthcare isn't waiting—it's already knocking. Are you ready to open the door?

Scan the QR code below with your phone's camera. This will direct you to open a web page that provides instant access to our comprehensive collection of free resources.

14

THE MEDICAL REVOLUTION IN ACTION

Two years ago, at 17 years old, Anna walked herself to the mailbox and back—independently, with forearm crutches, taking her time but moving with purpose and determination. As I watched her, I was struck by a profound realization: The 17-year-old young woman navigating our driveway was the same child doctors once told us would be a lifelong "vegetable." The same little girl who was never supposed to walk, talk or live independently was now planning her future with the kind of hope that medical professionals had declared impossible.

Anna's transformation isn't a miracle—it's medicine: precision-personalized medicine. It's the type of medicine that only comes from intense focus and deep research and is driven by unrelenting love. That's my girl! It's what happens when we stop accepting the limitations given to us and start addressing root causes. And she's not alone.

Across the country, in clinics, hospitals and even major medical institutions, a quiet revolution is taking place. Patients labeled "uncurable" are getting better. Conditions deemed "lifelong" are resolving. The impossible is becoming routine. This isn't happening in some distant future—it's happening right now, and the evidence is overwhelming.

More About Sarah's Journey: Unraveling the Mystery of Chronic Fatigue

Remember Sarah, who I first mentioned in Chapter Three? She came to my clinic carrying a thick folder of medical records and test results, the accumulated evidence of years spent searching for answers. At 35, she'd done everything "right"—eating well, exercising regularly, getting checkups—but her health had still collapsed.

Multiple doctors had run tests, prescribed medications and offered theories. Some said it was depression. Others suggested chronic fatigue syndrome. One doctor told her it was just "part of being a busy, stressed professional." None of their treatments helped. In fact, many made her feel worse.

When Sarah first walked into my office, I could see the desperation in her eyes. We were literally her clinic of last resort. She'd heard about functional medicine but wasn't sure if it could help where everything else had failed. What we discovered over the next several months would change her life completely.

The first breakthrough came through comprehensive testing that went far beyond standard blood work. We found multiple issues that had been completely missed:

Hidden thyroid dysfunction: While her TSH levels appeared "normal" on basic testing, a complete thyroid panel revealed the presence of thyroid antibodies, indicating Hashimoto's thyroiditis—an autoimmune condition affecting thyroid function. Remarkably, no previous doctor had bothered to test for this, despite autoimmune thyroid issues being incredibly common in women her age.

Environmental toxicity: Advanced testing revealed the effects of mycotoxins in her system—toxins produced by mold. Further investigation uncovered significant mold growth in her home, particularly in areas where she spent the most time. The chronic exposure was triggering systemic inflammation, activating her autoimmunity and compromising her detoxification pathways.

Gut and immune dysfunction: Specialized stool testing revealed small intestinal bacterial overgrowth (SIBO) and chronic inflammatory response syndrome (CIRS), both triggered by the mold exposure. Her gut, where 90 percent of serotonin is produced, was in chaos—explaining not just her physical symptoms but her mood issues as well.

Nutritional deficiencies: Despite eating what she thought was a healthy diet, Sarah was deficient in multiple key nutrients, including B vitamins, magnesium and omega-3 fatty acids—all critical for energy production and neurological function.

Addressing these root causes required a comprehensive approach. Sarah and her husband eventually moved from the mold-contaminated home, implemented a targeted detoxification protocol, healed her gut with specific therapeutic interventions, corrected her nutritional deficiencies and optimized her thyroid function with tailored hormone replacement.

The transformation was remarkable. Within three months, Sarah's energy began returning. Within six months, she felt better than she had in years. But the most extraordinary change came a year later—after several heartbreaking miscarriages and being told she had fertility issues, Sarah achieved something she'd almost given up hoping for: She became pregnant. Her body, once too compromised to sustain a pregnancy, was now thriving enough to create new life.

But perhaps most importantly, we didn't just treat her symptoms —we addressed the autoimmune process itself. By healing her gut, replenishing deficient nutrients and removing environmental toxins, we halted the progression of her previously undiagnosed autoimmune condition. Sarah didn't just get better; she got her life back.

Isaiah's Miracle: When the Impossible Becomes Possible

Some cases challenge everything we think we know about medicine and healing. Isaiah's story is one of those cases.

At three years old, Isaiah developed acute demyelinating encephalomyelitis (ADEM), a devastating condition where the immune system attacks the myelin sheaths protecting the brain's nerves. The resulting inflammation essentially shut down his neurological function. He lost his ability to speak, to interact and to engage with the world around him. In many ways, it was like autism, but worse—Isaiah's personality had simply disappeared.

His mother, struggling financially and barely scraping by on Medicaid, had nowhere else to turn. The conventional medical system had done what it could, but Isaiah remained locked inside himself, unreachable and unresponsive. When she brought him to see me in 2017, I could see the desperation in her eyes and the determination that only a mother fighting for her child can possess. My wife and I had been in the same situation before.

We implemented a comprehensive strategy built around what limited resources were available to this family. The foundation was the GAPS diet—a specialized nutritional protocol designed to heal the gut lining and reduce brain inflammation, particularly effective for brain-injured children. This wasn't expensive or complicated, but it was work; it involved using a Crock-Pot to prepare nutrient-dense, easily digestible meals that could support his healing process. This diet was created by Nathasha Campbell-McBride, MD, a Russian neurosurgeon, and it focuses on healing the brain through a focused gut rehabilitation.

We paired this with basic but targeted supplementation to address the severe nutrient deficiencies we uncovered through basic and functional lab tests. Additionally, we introduced low-dose naltrexone, an older medication that has been repurposed to help modulate the immune system, especially in cases involving autoimmune conditions. I frequently use it in patients with autism, and research supports its benefits in traumatic brain and spinal cord injuries.

The results didn't come overnight, but within a few months, something extraordinary began to happen. Isaiah's brain function started to return. His behavior stabilized. His personality began to resurface. And most incredibly—he began to speak again.

By nine months, Isaiah was "back." The child who had been written off by the medical system, whose brain had been devastated by autoimmune inflammation, had defied every expectation and prediction.

Isaiah's story proves a fundamental truth: The body's capacity for healing, even from seemingly irreversible damage, is far greater than conventional medicine acknowledges. When we provide the right support—even with limited resources—remarkable recoveries are possible.

Sheila's Breakthrough: The Power of Pattern Recognition

Sometimes the most profound insights come from the simplest observations. Sheila's case was one of my earliest lessons in functional medicine before I even started my official certification training, and it taught me something crucial about the power of therapeutic trials and patient education.

Sheila was in her mid-30s, battling chronic fatigue and fibromyalgia since her teens. Her lifestyle reflected the typical American habits of that time: She smoked, drank soda daily and ate a highly processed diet. Unsurprisingly, she felt terrible most of the time.

By then, I had already studied the critical connection between gut health, chronic constipation, yeast overgrowth and brain fog—ideas I had learned from Dr. Jacob Teitelbaum, a pioneer in chronic fatigue and fibromyalgia treatment ("Eliminating Candida Overgrowth," Teitelbaum, 2021). The research was compelling: Chronic yeast overgrowth in the gut could trigger systemic inflammation and neurological symptoms, and in some this could look like chronic fatigue syndrome. So I suggested something simple to Sheila: a one-week therapeutic trial of Diflucan, a medication that targets yeast overgrowth. If her symptoms were related to Candida, we should see improvement.

The results were eye-opening. After taking Diflucan for just one week, Sheila's chronic fatigue vanished for nearly two months. When her symptoms eventually returned, she came back asking for more of the medication.

This therapeutic trial had revealed something crucial: Sheila had Candida overgrowth syndrome, a condition that many conventional doctors don't recognize or treat. But here's where the story becomes instructive—and where I learned one of my most important lessons about functional medicine.

I explained to Sheila that while the Diflucan had been diagnostic and temporarily therapeutic, real and lasting improvement would require addressing the root causes that allowed the yeast overgrowth to develop in the first place. She needed to eliminate the refined sugars and processed foods that fed the yeast, cut out all soda, quit smoking (which compromises immune function) and make comprehensive lifestyle changes.

Unfortunately, Sheila only wanted another round of Diflucan. She wasn't ready for the deeper work that real healing required. I gave her another short round of Diflucan with the instructions to pick one thing to change and then come back in two to three months. I never saw her again, though three months later she did request another refill of the medicine.

This case taught me that functional medicine success depends on two equally important factors: correct diagnosis and treatment, and patient education and commitment. You can identify the root cause perfectly, but without patient engagement and lifestyle modification, the results won't last.

Sheila's case was both one of my first major successes and one of my first major lessons about the importance of comprehensive care, patient education and patient engagement in functional medicine.

The Global Perspective: Lessons from Traditional Wisdom

Sometimes the most powerful validation of functional medicine principles comes from unexpected sources. One of the most striking examples involves a landmark study from China that revolutionized our understanding of how simple nutritional interventions can have profound public health implications.

Researchers were investigating a viral infection called Keshan Disease that was causing heart disease in children throughout certain regions of China. A US pharmaceutical company was simultaneously developing an expensive vaccine to prevent this viral-induced cardiomyopathy, following the conventional medical approach of creating a drug to fight the disease.

But Chinese researchers discovered something far more elegant and effective: The virus was only able to cause heart disease in children who were deficient in selenium, an essential trace mineral. When the virus encountered selenium-deficient hosts, it mutated into more virulent forms that could damage heart tissue. However, children with adequate selenium levels were naturally protected—their bodies resisted the virus entirely ("An Original Discovery: Selenium Deficiency and Keshan Disease," Chen, 2012).

The solution was remarkably simple: selenium supplementation throughout the affected regions. The results were so definitive that the expensive vaccine development was abandoned. Instead of treating the disease after it occurred, they prevented it by addressing the underlying nutritional deficiency that made children vulnerable in the first place.

This example perfectly illustrates a fundamental principle of functional medicine: Small, targeted interventions that address root causes can often be more effective than complex medical treatments that focus on fighting disease after it develops.

Here are some other examples I've encountered in my travels outside the US: While working in a mission hospital in Shell, Ecuador, I would routinely see healthy young males develop something I had never seen in the US: deep muscle abscess in their thighs.

These usually occurred after some kind of trauma—usually while playing soccer. When I saw something similar in the US, it was usually in heroin or cocaine users after injecting with dirty needles. But in Ecuador, these were healthy, athletic young males. During my time there I learned that the diet, consisting of beans and rice, induced nutrient deficiencies, specifically in certain nutrients that made these athletes more prone to this infection.

I made a similar discovery while my family was studying Spanish in Tuis de Turialba, Costa Rica. We had decided to take a two-week holiday to immerse ourselves in the language and chose a rural, idyllic community. But when my teacher learned that I was a medical doctor, she started to ask me questions. I learned that this area was one of the top three areas in the world for gastric cancer. But why? I figured it out in a week.

Tuis de Turialba is an agricultural center—and in Costa Rica that means they spray lots of pesticides where they grow produce. There were two Walmart-sized stores in this small town where all they sold were chemicals and pesticides for the local farmers. On top of this, the local culture's diet included large amounts of seasoned, processed meats loaded with nitrates. Nitrates by themselves are associated with an increased risk of colon cancer. But on top of that, add all the chemicals, and you have the perfect storm for cancer.

The New Medical Reality

What connects all these stories—Anna's defiance of cerebral palsy predictions, Lizzy's recovery from misdiagnosed POTS, Sarah's emergence from chronic fatigue, Isaiah's return from neurological devastation, Sheila's temporary but revealing response to antifungal treatment and the selenium study's elegant prevention strategy—is a common thread: Conventional medicine had missed the mark, while functional medicine approaches found solutions.

These aren't isolated cases or rare exceptions. They represent a pattern that's becoming increasingly common as more practitioners and institutions embrace functional medicine principles. The revolution isn't coming—it's already here.

The difference lies in the approach. Conventional medicine asks: What disease does this patient have, and what medication treats that disease? Functional medicine asks: Why is this patient sick, and what does their body need to heal?

This shift in perspective—from disease management to health optimization—is transforming outcomes across the medical spectrum. When we address root causes instead of suppressing symptoms, when we support the body's natural healing mechanisms instead of overriding them, when we treat patients as unique individuals instead of collections of symptoms, extraordinary results become ordinary occurrences.

The stories in this chapter should be the norm, not the exception. Every patient deserves the kind of thorough investigation that uncovered Sarah's mold toxicity and thyroid dysfunction. Every teenager like Lizzy deserves proper testing for conditions like POTS before being dismissed with psychiatric labels. Every family like Isaiah's deserves access to the nutritional and therapeutic interventions that can support recovery from even devastating conditions.

The medical revolution isn't about rejecting conventional medicine—it's about expanding it. It's about combining the best of traditional medical knowledge with functional medicine insights, creating a more complete and effective approach to healing.

This revolution is happening in research institutions, clinical practices and, most importantly, in the lives of patients who refuse to accept "uncurable" as their final answer. The evidence is mounting, the outcomes are undeniable and the transformation of healthcare is accelerating.

The question isn't whether functional medicine works—these stories and countless others provide overwhelming evidence that it does. The question is how quickly we can make this approach available to everyone who needs it.

BECAUSE EVERY PERSON deserves the chance to experience their own medical revolution—to move from hopeless diagnosis to defying all the odds, just like Anna, Lizzy, Sarah, Isaiah and thousands of others who refused to accept limitations and found their path to healing.

The revolution is real. The evidence is clear. And it's transforming lives every single day.

Scan the QR code below with your phone's camera. This will direct you to open a web page that provides instant access to our comprehensive collection of free resources.

PART IV

YOUR TRANSFORMATION TOOLKIT

15

YOUR FOUNDATION FOR HEALING

Here's what I've learned after 25 years of clinical practice and over 100000 patient encounters: 80 percent of your healing potential comes from addressing just three core areas. I call this the "Triangle of Health," and it's the foundation that makes everything else possible.

Many people get lost in the complexity of health optimization—endless supplements, complicated protocols and expensive biohacks. But the truth is simpler and more powerful: Master these three fundamentals, and your body's natural ability to heal will kick into overdrive. Miss them, and no amount of advanced intervention will create lasting transformation.

This chapter contains everything you need to implement the systematic approach that has worked for thousands of my patients. These aren't theories or suggestions—they're proven protocols with specific dosages, clear instructions and measurable outcomes. By the time you finish this chapter, you'll have the foundations for your roadmap for transformation.

The Triangle of Health

AFTER ANALYZING the patterns across thousands of successful patient recoveries, three critical factors emerge consistently. Address these three areas effectively, and you'll experience the majority of your health improvements. Ignore them, and you'll struggle regardless of what other interventions you try.

1. Gut Health: Your Second Brain and Immune Command Center

Your gut isn't just for digestion—it's the headquarters of your immune system and the production center for 95 percent of your body's serotonin, 50 percent of dopamine and 75 percent of all brain neurotransmitters ("Associations of Neurotransmitters and the Gut Microbiome with Emotional Distress in Mixed-Type of Irritable Bowel Syndrome," Barandouzi et al., 2022). When your gut is compromised, everything else suffers: energy, mood, immunity, hormone balance and even cognitive function.

Here are some alarming statistics about the gut health crisis:

- 60 to 70 million Americans suffer from digestive diseases (National Institute of Diabetes and Digestive and Kidney Diseases, 2014).
- 70 percent of your immune system resides in your gut ("Regional Specialization Within the Intestinal Immune System," Mowat and Agace, 2014).
- Gut dysfunction is linked to depression, anxiety, autoimmune diseases and chronic fatigue ("Gut Instincts: Microbiota as a Key Regulator of Brain Development, Ageing and Neurodegeneration," Dinan and Cryan, 2016).
- Leaky gut syndrome affects an estimated 80 percent of people with chronic health conditions ("Leaky Gut: Mechanisms, Measurement and Clinical Implications in Humans," Camilleri, 2019).

When Sarah first came to see me, she had no idea that her crushing fatigue, brain fog and fertility struggles all traced back to the same source: her gut. Think of your gut as mission control for your entire body—when it's functioning optimally, you feel energized, think clearly and resist disease. When it's compromised, like Sarah's was, every system suffers. The good news? You can restore gut health by addressing these four critical areas that most doctors never even evaluate:

Food Reactivity and Inflammation

The Standard American Diet creates chronic inflammation through processed foods, industrial seed oils and hidden food sensitivities. Common culprits include gluten, dairy, corn, soy and eggs—but individual reactions vary significantly.

Bacterial Imbalance (Dysbiosis)

Your gut contains trillions of bacteria that should work in harmony. Antibiotics, stress, poor diet and environmental toxins disrupt this balance, leading to harmful bacteria overgrowth and beneficial bacteria depletion.

Intestinal Permeability (Leaky Gut)

When the gut lining becomes damaged, toxins and undigested food particles leak into the bloodstream, triggering widespread inflammation and autoimmune reactions.

Detoxification Pathways

Your gut plays a crucial role in eliminating toxins. When compromised, toxins recirculate, creating systemic inflammation and blocking healing processes.

2. Stress: The Hidden Saboteur of Health

Stress isn't just feeling overwhelmed—it's a complex physiological state that can block your body's ability to heal. This includes obvious acute stressors like trauma and PTSD but also chronic daily stressors like work pressure and relationship conflicts and even hidden stressors like blood sugar instability, chronic infections and unresolved trauma.

There is a direct connection between stress, its interpretation in your brain and nervous system and how that interconnects with your mind, immune system, hormones and even gut. This new field of study is called *psychoneuroimmunoendocrinology*. It's a long word that says it *IS* all in your head, but not the way you think.

- Chronic stress elevates cortisol, disrupting sleep, metabolism and immune function ("Restricted and Disrupted Sleep: Effects on Autonomic Function, Neuroendocrine Stress Systems and Stress Responsivity," Meerlo et al., 2008).
- Trauma literally rewires your nervous system, keeping you stuck in fight-or-flight mode ("Physiology and Neurobiology of Stress and Adaptation: Central Role of the Brain," McEwen, 2007).
- Even low-level chronic stressors act like trauma, preventing your body from entering healing states.
- Stress affects gene expression, turning on inflammatory pathways and turning off repair mechanisms ("The Emerging Field of Human Social Genomics," Slavich and Cole, 2013).
- This dysfunction is controlled through the interaction of your nervous system, hormonal system, immune system and your gut ("Gut Instincts: Microbiota as a Key Regulator of Brain Development, Ageing and Neurodegeneration," Dinan and Cryan, 2017).

Here's what most people don't realize: The stress that's sabotaging your health isn't always the obvious kind you feel in your mind. Your body experiences stress in three distinct ways, and each one can completely derail your healing—even when you're doing everything else perfectly. I see patients all the time who are frustrated because their healthy diet and expensive supplements aren't working. Nine times out of 10, it's because they're unknowingly dealing with chronic stress in one of these three categories. Understanding which type is affecting you is the key to breaking through healing plateaus:

Physical Stress:

- Poor sleep quality
- Blood sugar instability
- Chronic pain or inflammation
- Environmental toxins
- Nutritional deficiencies

Emotional Stress:

- Unresolved trauma
- Chronic anxiety or depression
- Relationship conflicts
- Financial pressure
- Work-related stress

Biochemical Stress:

- Hormone imbalances
- Chronic infections
- Food sensitivities
- Medication side effects
- Toxin exposure

3. Sleep: Your Body's Master Reset Button

The third point in the "Triangle of Health" is sleep. Sleep isn't just about feeling rested—it's literally when your body performs its most critical healing and detoxification processes. Think of sleep as your body's overnight maintenance crew. While you're unconscious, your brain is washing away toxic waste products, your immune system is ramping up to fight infections, your muscles are repairing microscopic damage and your hormones are resetting for the next day. Poor sleep quality doesn't just make you tired—it disrupts every single system in your body and can completely sabotage even the best nutrition and lifestyle interventions.

I see this constantly in my practice. Patients come in frustrated because they're eating perfectly, taking all the right supplements and still feeling awful. When we dig into their sleep patterns, we often find the missing piece: They're only getting five to six hours of fragmented sleep and wondering why their body can't heal.

The numbers are staggering, and they explain why so many people struggle with chronic health issues:

- The average American sleeps just six hours per night— compared to the eight and a half hours our great-grandparents averaged 150 years ago ("FastStats: Sleep in Adults," Center for Disease Control, 2024).
- 50 to 70 million Americans suffer from diagnosable sleep disorders, but millions more have poor sleep quality without realizing it ("Sleep Health," National Heart, Lung, and Blood Institute).
- Poor sleep increases your risk of diabetes, heart disease, obesity and cognitive decline by 40 to 60 percent, making it one of the most dangerous lifestyle factors you can't ignore ("Sleep Duration and All-Cause Mortality: A Systematic Review and Meta-Analysis of Prospective Studies," Cappuccio et al., 2010).
- Sleep deprivation disrupts hormone production (including insulin, cortisol and growth hormone), weakens immune function and literally prevents cellular repair processes from occurring ("Restricted and Disrupted Sleep: Effects on Autonomic Function,

Neuroendocrine Stress Systems and Stress Responsivity,"
Meerlo et al., 2008).

Here's what most people don't realize: You can't supplement your
way out of sleep deprivation. You can't exercise your way out of it. You
can't eat your way out of it. When sleep is broken, everything else
becomes much harder to fix.

Sleep isn't just about feeling rested—it's when your body
performs critical healing and detoxification processes. But not all
sleep is created equal. After working with thousands of patients, I've
identified the key markers that determine whether you're getting
truly restorative sleep or just spending time unconscious. Poor sleep
quality disrupts every system in your body and can sabotage even the
best nutrition and lifestyle interventions. Here are the four critical
areas I evaluate to determine if your sleep is actually supporting your
health or silently undermining it:

1. **Sleep initiation:** How quickly you fall asleep reflects your
   nervous system's ability to shift from alert to rest mode.
2. **Sleep maintenance:** Frequent awakening indicates
   underlying stress, hormone imbalances or blood sugar
   instability.
3. **Sleep efficiency:** The percentage of time in bed actually
   spent sleeping; poor efficiency suggests sleep architecture
   problems, often from mitochondrial dysfunction.
4. **Morning recovery:** How refreshed you feel upon waking
   indicates whether you achieved adequate deep and REM
   sleep cycles. Does it take one to two hours to wake up or
   do you wake up ready to tackle the day?

16

CORRECTING DEFICIENCIES

L et's address the nutritional crisis hiding in plain sight. Even people eating "healthy" diets often have critical deficiencies that block healing. Nutrient deficiencies actually fall under the gut section of the "Triangle of Health," but I pulled it out here because it is so important and often overlooked. And if you have nutrient deficiencies, your body systems can remain depleted and out of sync.

There is a deficiency epidemic. Here are some staggering statistics:

- 50 percent of Americans are deficient in magnesium—critical for over 300 enzymatic reactions ("Micronutrient Inadequacies in the US Population: An Overview," Drake and Frei, 2018).
- Up to 90 percent are deficient in potassium—essential for cellular function and blood pressure regulation (Drake and Frei).
- 40 to 60 percent are deficient in at least one B vitamin—crucial for energy production and neurological function.

Which means everyone has at least one B vitamin
deficiency and most have several (Drake and Frei).

- 70 percent have suboptimal vitamin D levels—vital for
  immune function and hormone regulation—and 40
  percent have gross deficiency (Drake and Frei).
- Up to 70 percent of Americans don't consume adequate
  omega-3 fatty acids—essential for brain health and
  inflammation control ("U.S. Adults are Not Meeting
  Recommended Levels for Fish and Omega-3 Fatty Acid
  Intake: Results of an Analysis Using Observational Data
  from NHANES 2003–2008," Papanikolaou et al., 2014).

The question I often hear is how can this be happening here in
the US, the richest country in the world? But a quick explanation
shows how pervasive the causes for nutritional deficiencies are in
our country.

- **Food processing:** Refining grains removes up to 80
  percent of nutrients. Standard food processing destroys
  healthy fats and antioxidant vitamins, and 60 percent of
  the foods we eat are ultraprocessed ("Effect of Primary
  Processing of Cereals and Legumes on its Nutritional
  Quality: A Comprehensive Review," Oghbaei et al., 2015;
  "Ultra-Processed Products are Becoming Dominant in the
  Global Food System," Monteiro et al., 2013).
- **Soil depletion:** Modern farming has reduced mineral
  content by 40 to 60 percent ("Dirt Poor: Have Fruits and
  Vegetables Become Less Nutritious?," Scheer and
  Moss, 2011).
- **Chemical exposure:** Pesticides and toxins increase our
  nutritional needs to combat these chemicals ("Impact of
  Micronutrient Supplementation on Pesticide Residual,
  Acetylcholinesterase Activity, and Oxidative Stress Among
  Farm Children Exposed to Pesticides," Medithi et al., 2022).

- **Stress:** Chronic stress depletes B vitamins, magnesium and vitamin C, and 60 to 70 percent of Americans are dealing with chronic stress ("Magnesium Status and Stress: The Vicious Circle Concept Revisited," Pickering et al., 2020; "Stress in America™ 2023: A Nation Grappling with Psychological Impacts of Collective Trauma," American Psychological Association, 2023).
- **Medications:** Many drugs deplete specific nutrients, and two-thirds of Americans take at least one medication ("Prevalence of Prescription Medications With Depression as a Potential Adverse Effect Among Adults in the United States," Qato et al., 2018).

Core Supplementation Protocol

Based on clinical experience with thousands of patients and informed by up-to-date research, I recommend these supplements to address the most common deficiencies and provide the foundation for healing:

Essential Daily Foundation:

Vitamin D3: 2000 to 5000 IU daily

- Supports immune function, bone health and hormone production
- Take with K2 for optimal calcium utilization
- Test levels annually; optimal range: 60-80 ng/mL

Magnesium glycinate: 400 to 600 mg daily

- Improves sleep quality and stress resilience
- Supports muscle and nerve function
- Take at bedtime for best absorption and sleep benefits

- Glycinate form is best absorbed and least likely to cause digestive upset

Omega-3 fish oil: 2000 to 3000 mg daily

- Reduces inflammation throughout the body
- Supports brain health and mood stability
- Choose molecularly distilled, third-party-tested brands
- Look for EPA:DHA ratio of 1:1, 2:1 or 3:1

Multi vitamin w/ B-complex (high-quality methylated forms) and minerals

- Supports energy production and nervous system function
- Look for methylfolate and methylcobalamin forms
- Take in the morning to avoid sleep interference

Vitamin C: 1000 to 2000 mg daily

- Powerful antioxidant and immune system support
- Supports collagen production and wound healing
- Buffered forms are gentler on the stomach

Advanced Therapeutic Supplements

Due to toxins in the environment, chemicals, mitochondrial dysfunction and general inflammation, the following could be considered for add-ons to boost cell function and recovery.

Curcumin: 1000 mg daily

- Powerful anti-inflammatory and brain health support
- Choose forms with enhanced bioavailability (like CurcuWin or BCM-95)
- Best taken with black pepper extract for absorption

Creatine: five grams daily

- Improves cellular energy production and cognitive function
- Supports muscle health and exercise performance
- One of the most researched and safest supplements available

NMN (nicotinamide mononucleotide): 500 to 1000 mg daily

- Supports cellular energy production and longevity pathways
- May help reverse aspects of aging at the cellular level
- Best taken in the morning on an empty stomach

Resveratrol: 500 to 1000 mg daily

- Activates longevity genes and provides antioxidant protection
- Supports cardiovascular health and brain function
- Choose trans-resveratrol for best bioavailability

Low-dose naltrexone (LDN): 1.5 to 4.5 mg nightly

- This one is a simple biohack due to its immune modulating effects and how it balances the three arms of the adaptive immune system (Th1, Th2 and Tregs). It's great for autoimmune conditions and immune-related inflammation.
- Modulates immune system and reduces inflammation
- Helpful for autoimmune conditions, chronic fatigue and chronic pain
- Requires prescription from knowledgeable physician
- Research shows benefits for long COVID, autism, SIBO and multiple sclerosis

17

BIOHACKING TOOLS: OPTIMIZING YOUR BIOLOGY

A lot of people are wary of alternative treatments and worry about whether they're safe or not. Your concern is smart. Not all alternative methods are equal. But don't forget that traditional medicine also has risks, maybe bigger risks. You need to learn all the options so you can make the best decisions possible. You need to become a health detective. Before you agree to a treatment, make sure you're able to give true informed consent (which can't be delivered after a quick 60 second explanation). Ask for studies on any treatment you're considering. Talk to people who've tried it. Here's the thing: Even "proven" treatments have risks. The key is making informed choices. Trust your gut and say no if something doesn't feel right.

The nice thing about many alternative treatments and biohacking is that they don't require expensive equipment or extreme measures. These evidence-based tools can dramatically improve your health outcomes.

Here are some basic biohacks—no equipment required:

Intermittent fasting:

- Start with 12-hour eating window; progress to eight to 10 hours
- Improves insulin sensitivity and cellular cleanup (autophagy)
- Begin gradually to avoid stress on your system

Cold exposure:

- End showers with 30 to 60 seconds of cold water
- Activates brown fat, improves circulation and boosts metabolism
- Builds stress resilience and immune function

Heat therapy:

- Sauna sessions 15 to 20 minutes, three to four times weekly
- Improves cardiovascular health and promotes detoxification
- Infrared saunas offer benefits at lower temperatures

Breathwork:

- Box breathing: four counts in, hold for four, out for four, hold for four
- Activates parasympathetic nervous system and reduces stress
- Practice five to 10 minutes daily for optimal benefits

HERE ARE some more advanced biohacking tools that require a purchase or locating a facility in a nearby community that provides the service:

Neuromuscular stimulation (NMS) devices:

- TENS units, PowerDot or Revitive circulation boosters
- Improve muscle tone, circulation and neurological function
- 15 to 30 minutes daily; particularly effective for neurological conditions

Red light therapy:

- 660 to 850nm wavelengths for 10 to 20 minutes daily
- Supports cellular energy production and wound healing
- Helpful for skin health, muscle recovery and inflammation

Heart rate variability (HRV) monitoring:

- Track nervous system recovery and stress resilience
- Devices like HeartMath or Oura Ring provide real-time feedback
- Use data to optimize training, stress management and recovery

Grounding/earthing:

- Direct skin contact with earth for 20 to 30 minutes daily
- Reduces inflammation and improves sleep quality
- Free and accessible—walk barefoot on grass, sand or soil

Detoxification Protocols: Clearing the Obstacles to Healing

MODERN LIFE EXPOSES us to thousands of toxins that our ancestors never encountered. Supporting your body's natural detoxification processes is essential for optimal health.

Here are some gentle daily detox methods that will support your health recovery:

Hydration:

- Drink half your body weight in ounces of filtered water daily
- Add trace minerals or sea salt for optimal hydration
- Filter out chlorine, fluoride and other contaminants

Liver support:

- Milk thistle: 200 to 400 mg daily
- N-acetylcysteine (NAC): 600 to 1200 mg daily
- Support phases one and two liver detoxification pathways

Lymphatic support:

- Dry brushing before showers
- Gentle bouncing or rebounding
- Stay hydrated and move regularly

Here are some more advanced detox interventions that will support wellness:

Sauna therapy:

- Promotes elimination of fat-soluble toxins through sweat
- Start with 10 to 15 minutes; build to 20 to 30 minutes
- Ensure adequate hydration and electrolyte replacement

Coffee enemas:

- Support liver detoxification and energy production
- Use organic, light-roast coffee
- Consult an experienced practitioner for proper technique

Castor oil packs:

- Apply to abdomen for liver and digestive support
- Use two to three times weekly for 45 to 60 minutes
- Promotes lymphatic drainage and reduces inflammation

18

HEALTH TRACKING: MEASURING YOUR PROGRESS

W hat gets measured gets managed. Proper tracking helps you identify patterns, measure progress and optimize your protocols. Here are some essential health metrics:

Daily tracking:

- Energy levels (one to 10 scale)
- Sleep quality and duration
- Mood and mental clarity
- Digestive function
- Pain or symptom severity

Weekly assessments:

- Weight and body composition
- Exercise performance and recovery
- Stress levels and coping ability
- Overall well-being score

Monthly evaluations:

- Progress toward health goals
- Protocol effectiveness
- Supplement needs assessment
- Lifestyle optimization opportunities

Health Journaling System

Daily Entry Format:

Date: _____
Sleep: Quality (one to 10) __ Duration: __ hours
Energy: Morning __ Afternoon __ Evening __
Mood: (one to 10) __
Symptoms: _____
Food: Breakfast: _____
Lunch: _____
Dinner: _____
Snacks: _____
Exercise: _____
Supplements: _____
Notes: _____

Weekly Review Questions:

- What patterns am I noticing?
- Which interventions seem most helpful?
- What challenges did I face this week?
- What adjustments should I make?
- What victories can I celebrate?

Food as Medicine: Your Nutritional Prescription
The right food choices can be more powerful than medications

for many chronic conditions. Here's how to optimize your nutrition   for healing:

Anti-Inflammatory Foundation Foods

Prioritize these daily:

- **Leafy greens:** Spinach, kale, arugula—rich in folate and antioxidants
- **Colorful vegetables:** Bell peppers, carrots, beets—provide diverse phytonutrients
- **Healthy fats:** Avocados, olive oil, nuts, seeds—support hormone production
- **Quality proteins:** Grass-fed meats, wild-caught fish, pasture-raised eggs
- **Fermented foods:** Sauerkraut, kimchi, kefir—support gut health

Eliminate these inflammatory foods:

- **Processed vegetable oils:** Canola, soybean, corn oil—promote inflammation
- **Refined sugars:** High fructose corn syrup, processed sweets
- **Processed grains:** White bread, crackers, cereals
- **Artificial additives:** Food dyes, preservatives, artificial sweeteners

Therapeutic Dietary Approaches

For gut healing—GAPS Diet:

- Focuses on healing and sealing the gut lining
- Emphasizes bone broth, fermented foods and easily digestible nutrients

- Eliminates grains, processed foods and refined sugars
- Particularly effective for autism, autoimmune conditions, and digestive disorders

For food sensitivity—Elimination Diet:

- Remove common triggers for three to four weeks: gluten, dairy, eggs, soy, corn, nuts
- Systematically reintroduce foods to identify specific reactions
- Track symptoms carefully during reintroduction phase

For digestive issues—Low FODMAP:

- Reduces fermentable carbohydrates that can trigger SIBO symptoms
- Temporary protocol (four to six weeks) followed by systematic reintroduction
- Work with knowledgeable practitioner for best results

Food Sourcing Excellence

Quality matters as much as quantity when it comes to nutrition. Here's how to source the most nutrient-dense, healing foods:

Protein sources:

- **Grass-fed/grass-finished beef:** Higher omega-3s, conjugated linoleic acid
- **Pasture-raised poultry:** Better nutrient profile, no antibiotics/hormones
- **Wild-caught fish:** Lower mercury, higher omega-3 content
- **Pasture-raised eggs:** Higher vitamin D, omega-3s and beta-carotene

Produce priority:

Use the Environmental Working Group's "Dirty Dozen" and "Clean Fifteen" lists to prioritize organic purchases:

- **Always buy organic:** Strawberries, spinach, kale, peaches, pears, nectarines, apples, grapes, bell peppers, celery, tomatoes, potatoes
- **Conventional okay:** Avocados, sweet corn, pineapple, onions, papaya, frozen sweet peas, asparagus, honeydew, kiwi, cabbage, mushrooms, mangoes, sweet potatoes, watermelon, carrots

Fats and oils:

- **Extra virgin olive oil:** Cold-pressed, in dark glass bottles
- **Coconut oil:** Organic, unrefined, cold-pressed
- **Avocado oil:** High heat cooking, cold-pressed
- **Grass-fed butter:** Rich in vitamins A, K2 and CLA

19

TECH TOOLS

The coolest part about healthcare's future is that technology is making it available to everyone, not just rich people. Technology makes everything easier and cheaper.

Your Phone Becomes Your Health Assistant

Apps can now analyze your symptoms quicker than many doctors. You type in how you're feeling, and the app suggests what might be wrong and whether you need to see a doctor right away.

Your lab results get analyzed by computers that can spot patterns humans miss. They can predict health problems before you even feel sick.

Nutrition apps tell you exactly what to eat based on your genes and how your body reacts to different foods.

Wearable Devices Track Everything

Heart rate monitors like Oura Ring or Apple Watch can tell if you're stressed, recovered from yesterday's workout or getting sick before you feel symptoms.

Sleep trackers show you exactly what's happening while you sleep and how to sleep better.

Continuous glucose monitors (originally just for diabetics) now help healthy people figure out which foods give them energy and which ones make them crash.

Air quality monitors in your home alert you to mold, pollution or chemicals that could be making you sick.

See Doctors From Anywhere

Video appointments mean you can see functional medicine doctors from anywhere in the world. You're not stuck with whatever doctors happen to be in your town.

Home lab tests let you get comprehensive health testing without going to a lab. Companies mail you test kits, and you get results with doctor explanations online.

20

INVESTING YOUR MONEY IN YOUR HEALTH

Here's the reality about healthcare costs that everyone should understand—the numbers are honestly shocking:

- Healthcare expenditures per person in the US are over $13000 per year ("How Much is Health Spending Expected to Grow?," McGough et al., 2024).
- If you have insurance through work, you still pay about $1500 out of pocket each year.
- Your family probably pays over $6000 toward insurance premiums.
- Emergency room visits cost $2000 to $10000 each time.
- 90 percent of all healthcare spending goes to treating chronic diseases ("National Health Expenditure Projections 2015-2025," Centers for Medicare and Medicaid Services).

Why Prevention Saves Money

Here's what most people don't realize: **Spending money to stay healthy costs way less than treating disease.**

- Spend $1 on nutrition coaching, save $3 to $7 on medical bills later.
- Spend $1 on stress management, save $2 to $4 on medications.
- Spend $1 on finding root causes, save $10 to $50 on unnecessary procedures.

Instead of waiting to get sick and then spending huge amounts on treatment, smart people invest in:

- **One thorough functional medicine evaluation** ($2000 to $5000) that often prevents decades of doctor visits and medications
- **Nutrition coaching** ($1000 to $3000 per year) that prevents diseases costing $50000+ to treat
- **Stress management therapy** ($2000 to $5000 per year) that prevents mental health crises costing $20000+ to fix

New Ways To Pay for Healthcare

Smart people are finding ways around the traditional insurance system:

Direct primary care lets you pay your doctor directly ($50 to $200 per month) and skip insurance for basic care. You get unlimited visits and your doctor actually has time to talk to you.

Concierge medicine gives you a personal relationship with a doctor who knows you well and focuses on prevention.

21

HOW YOU CAN HELP CHANGE HEALTHCARE

E very choice you make influences the future of medicine. When you choose functional medicine doctors, you create demand for doctors who look for root causes instead of just prescribing pills.

When you invest in your health before getting sick, you show insurance companies that prevention works and costs less. When you share your success story, you help friends and family learn about better options.

Your health transformation affects everyone around you:

- Your family sees you feeling better and wants the same thing.
- Your friends notice you have more energy and ask what you're doing.
- Your coworkers see you taking fewer sick days.
- People on social media learn from your posts about health improvements.

This creates a chain reaction. Every person you influence goes on to influence others. Your individual choice can eventually reach thousands of people.

What Your Future Healthcare Could Look Like

Imagine visiting your doctor five years from now:

Before your appointment, your doctor already reviewed data from your fitness tracker, recent lab tests and the air quality monitor in your home. A computer analyzed everything and suggested what to focus on.

During your 90-minute visit, your doctor talks with you about your health goals and adjusts your personalized plan. No rushing. No feeling like just another number.

Your meal plan is designed specifically for your genes and how your body processes different foods. You know exactly what to eat for optimal energy and health.

Your exercise program changes based on how well you're recovering, your stress levels and your goals. An app coaches you through workouts and corrects your form.

Your mental health support includes both human therapists and AI apps available 24/7 for support and crisis help.

Your total healthcare costs are lower than today because you're staying healthy instead of treating diseases after they develop.

This isn't science fiction. Everything I just described exists right now. The question is how quickly you'll decide to access it.

Why Change Is Happening So Fast

Several factors are making healthcare change faster than ever. First, too many people—six out of 10 adults—have chronic diseases ("Combating America's Chronic Disease Epidemic," Abir, 2025; "Trends in Multiple Chronic Conditions Among US Adults, By Life Stage, Behavioral Risk Factor Surveillance System, 2013–2023," Watson et al., 2025). Second, healthcare costs are rising faster than people can afford. Third, doctors are burning out and leaving traditional practice. And lastly, young people expect personalized care like they get from Netflix or Amazon, and technology makes all this possible: Smartphones put powerful health tools in everyone's hands, AI can analyze health data better than humans, genetic testing costs less than $500 and social media spreads new information within days.

Another reason for rapid change is that employers realize healthy workers are more productive and cost less. Insurance companies discover prevention costs less than treatment, and individuals understand that investing in health saves money in the long term. The economics finally make sense.

The future of medicine is here right now, but it's not available everywhere yet. Some people are already living with this new kind of healthcare while others are stuck in the old system. The difference isn't money or special connections. It's knowledge and willingness to take charge of your health. You can wait for your current doctor to change, or you can find practitioners who already practice this way. You can hope insurance will cover better care someday, or you can invest in your health now as the foundation for everything else in your life. You can keep doing the same things and hope for different results, or you can become one of the early adopters who gets the best healthcare available.

The doctor of the future is the patient—and that's you. The future of medicine is here. The only question is whether you're ready to claim it.

Your health is too important to leave to chance. The tools for feeling amazing are too good to ignore. Every choice you make, every dollar you spend on health, every doctor you choose is a vote for the kind of healthcare you want. Stop waiting for someone else to fix the system. Start building your own path to optimal health today.

You Are Your Advocate

Nobody cares about your health as much as you do.

That's not cynicism—it's reality. And once you accept this truth, it becomes incredibly empowering. After witnessing thousands of patient interactions over 25 years, I've observed a clear pattern: Patients who take ownership of their healthcare journey consistently achieve better outcomes than those who passively defer to authority.

This isn't about becoming your own doctor or rejecting medical expertise. It's about becoming an informed, organized and strategic partner in your own care. The patients who master these skills don't just get better treatment—they often discover solutions that the system missed entirely.

22

THE STRATEGIC MINDSET: THINKING LIKE A CEO

Think of yourself as the CEO of a company called "Your Health, Inc." You wouldn't run a business without understanding your finances, tracking performance metrics or building strategic partnerships. Your health deserves the same level of attention and organization.

As CEO, your responsibilities include:

- **Strategic planning:** Setting health goals and creating actionable plans
- **Team building:** Assembling the right mix of healthcare professionals
- **Quality control:** Monitoring outcomes and adjusting strategies
- **Risk management:** Identifying potential problems before they become crises
- **Performance tracking:** Measuring progress against defined objectives

This mindset shift—from passive patient to active CEO—changes everything about how you interact with the healthcare system.

Building Your Board of Directors: The Power of Multiple Perspectives

In business, successful CEOs surround themselves with advisors who bring different expertise and perspectives. Your health requires the same multifaceted approach.

The Functional Primary Care Strategist: Merging Functional and Conventional Medicine

This person serves as your chief operating officer—someone who understands your overall health picture and can coordinate complex care. Look for providers who:

- Schedule adequate time for complex discussions (45+ minutes for comprehensive visits)
- Ask about your health goals, not just your symptoms
- Understand both conventional and integrative approaches
- Maintain relationships with diverse specialists
- Respond to your communications promptly and thoughtfully

The unfortunate reality is that not everyone has access to one of these. The rest of this chapter gives you tools to help navigate this reality.

Interview Questions for Potential Primary Care Providers:

- How do you approach chronic conditions that don't respond to standard treatments?
- Are you comfortable working with functional medicine practitioners?
- How do you handle cases where multiple specialists provide conflicting advice?

- What's your philosophy about patient involvement in treatment decisions?

The Functional Medicine Detective

For complex chronic conditions, you need someone trained to investigate root causes rather than just manage symptoms. These providers should:

- Order comprehensive testing beyond standard panels
- Understand environmental medicine and toxic exposures
- Recognize the gut-brain-immune system connections
- Have experience with therapeutic nutrition and lifestyle medicine
- Offer personalized protocols based on individual biochemistry

Red Flags When Evaluating Functional Medicine Practitioners:

- Promises of miraculous cures
- One-size-fits-all protocols regardless of individual needs
- Excessive supplement sales without clear rationale
- Dismissal of all conventional medicine
- Unwillingness to work with your other providers

The Communication Specialist

Mental health and stress management aren't luxury add-ons— they're essential components of any comprehensive health strategy. Seek providers who:

- Understand trauma-informed care and its physical manifestations
- Recognize the bidirectional relationship between mental and physical health

- Offer evidence-based therapies like EMDR, somatic experiencing or cognitive-behavioral therapy
- Can address both acute mental health crises and long-term emotional wellness

The Movement and Recovery Team

Physical health extends far beyond medical treatments. Your movement team might include:

- **Physical therapists** with advanced manual therapy training
- **Massage therapists** specializing in medical or therapeutic massage
- **Personal trainers** with knowledge of therapeutic exercise and rehabilitation
- **Bodyworkers** trained in techniques like craniosacral therapy or myofascial release

Documentation Revolution: Your Personal Health Intelligence System

Effective advocacy requires superior documentation. Your records should be so comprehensive and well organized that any provider can quickly understand your health history, current status and treatment responses.

Creating Your Health Command Center

The Summary Page

This page is an overview and summary of all your previous diagnoses, surgeries and treatments chronologically on one page in one place. This allows anyone to get a quick 10000-foot view of your health history. You will update it regularly so your team has all the info they need to see in one place.

The Master Timeline

Create a chronological health history that includes:

- Major life events (births, deaths, divorces, job changes, moves)
- Significant health events (injuries, surgeries, major illnesses)
- Environmental exposures (mold, chemicals, infections)
- Medication and supplement history with dates and responses
- Stress events and their correlation with health changes

The Provider Portfolio

Maintain detailed records for each healthcare provider:

- Contact information and office procedures
- Specialties and training background
- Your assessment of their strengths and limitations
- Communication preferences and response times
- Billing and insurance coordination efficiency

The Intervention Log

Track every health intervention with:

- Start and stop dates
- Specific dosages or protocols
- Measurable outcomes (energy, pain and sleep)
- Side effects or unexpected responses
- Cost and insurance coverage

- Overall assessment of effectiveness

Advanced Tracking Strategies

Symptom Pattern Analysis

Create detailed logs that can reveal hidden connections:

- Time of day patterns
- Seasonal correlations
- Food and symptom relationships
- Sleep quality impacts
- Stress triggers and health responses
- Environmental factor influences

Treatment Response Mapping

For each intervention, track:

- Immediate responses (within days)
- Short-term effects (two to four weeks)
- Long-term outcomes (three-plus months)
- Sustainability of improvements
- Need for ongoing support or adjustments

Communication

The quality of your communication directly influences the quality of care you receive. Strategic communication isn't about being demanding—it's about being clear, prepared and purposeful.

Pre-Appointment Strategy

The Executive Brief

PREPARE A ONE-PAGE DOCUMENT THAT INCLUDES:

- Chief concerns (maximum of three)
- Relevant timeline since last visit
- Current treatments and their effects
- Specific questions requiring answers
- Your goals for this appointment

The Research Summary

If you've found relevant research or treatment options:

- Summarize key points in two to three sentences
- Include credible sources
- Frame as curiosity, not demands: "I came across this study about [condition]. I'm curious about your thoughts on this approach."

The Decision Framework

Before major treatment decisions, prepare:

- Your understanding of the problem
- Your treatment goals and priorities
- Your risk tolerance
- Your questions about alternatives
- Your timeline for making decisions

During-Appointment Tactics

The Three-Question Rule

Prioritize your most important questions and ask them early:

- The most critical concern or decision
- The most puzzling or confusing aspect
- The most important next step

The Clarification Loop

When receiving complex information:

- "Let me make sure I understand correctly..."
- "So what you're saying is..."
- "How does this relate to [previous concern]?"
- "What would this mean for my daily life?"

The Collaboration Frame

Position requests as partnership opportunities:

- "I'd like to work with you to understand..."
- "What additional information would help you help me?"
- "How can I best support the treatment plan?"
- "What should I watch for that might indicate progress or problems?"

Post-Appointment Follow-Up

The Summary Email

Within 24 hours, send a brief recap:

- Your understanding of key points discussed
- Agreed-upon next steps
- Any clarification needs
- Appreciation for their time and expertise

The Action Plan

Create specific, measurable steps based on your appointment:

- What you'll do before the next visit
- What you'll track or monitor
- When you'll follow up
- What would trigger an earlier contact

Navigating System Failures

Sometimes, despite your best efforts at strategic advocacy, the system fails. Knowing how to escalate effectively can prevent minor problems from becoming major crises.

Early Warning System

Documentation Red Flags:

- Conflicting information in medical records
- Lost test results or failure to follow up on abnormal findings
- Medication errors or dangerous drug interactions
- Communication breakdowns between providers
- Billing irregularities that suggest documentation problems

Provider Performance Red Flags:

- Consistent lateness or frequent appointment cancellations
- Defensive responses to reasonable questions
- Unwillingness to coordinate with other team members
- Failure to return calls or respond to urgent concerns
- Dismissive attitude toward your symptoms or research

Escalation Strategies

Level 1: Direct Provider Communication

- Schedule a dedicated appointment to address concerns
- Bring written documentation of specific issues
- Request specific changes or improvements
- Set clear timelines for resolution

Level 2: Practice Management

- Contact office managers or patient coordinators
- Request patient advocate involvement
- Document all communications in writing
- Seek alternative providers within the same system

Building Resilience: The Multiple Option Strategy

Never rely on a single provider for critical decisions:

- Maintain relationships with backup providers
- Know where to get urgent care in your area
- Keep updated medication and allergy lists accessible
- Prepare for provider transitions or practice closures

The Emergency Preparedness Plan

Create detailed instructions for health emergencies:

- Current medication list with dosages
- Key contact information for all providers
- Summary of major health conditions and treatments
- Clear directives for emergency care preferences
- Designated health decision-makers if you're incapacitated

The Long-Term Vision: Advocacy as Personal Evolution

EFFECTIVE HEALTH ADVOCACY isn't just about solving current problems —it's about developing the skills and systems that serve your lifelong well-being.

Continuous Improvement Strategies

Quarterly Reviews

Every three months, assess:

- Progress toward health goals
- Effectiveness of current providers
- Quality of your documentation system
- Communication skills development
- Areas needing additional support

Annual Strategic Planning

Once yearly, conduct a comprehensive review:

- Update health goals based on new circumstances
- Evaluate team performance and make changes
- Review insurance options and coverage needs
- Plan preventive care and health optimization
- Assess emergency preparedness plans

Skills Development

Continuously improve your advocacy capabilities:

- Learn about new developments in your health conditions
- Practice communication techniques
- Expand your provider network

- Refine your documentation systems
- Build relationships with other informed patients

Teaching and Mentoring

Sharing Your Expertise

As you develop advocacy skills:

- Help friends and family improve their healthcare experiences
- Mentor newly diagnosed patients
- Participate in patient education programs
- Provide feedback to healthcare organizations
- Write reviews and recommendations for excellent providers

Systemic Change

Use your voice to improve healthcare for everyone:

- Participate in patient advisory committees
- Provide feedback on quality improvement initiatives
- Support healthcare reform efforts
- Vote for candidates who prioritize patient-centered care
- Advocate for transparency in healthcare pricing and outcomes

23

YOUR 30-DAY IMPLEMENTATION PLAN

Remember: This isn't about perfection—it's about progress. Start where you are, use what you have and do what you can. Your body has an incredible capacity for healing when given the right support. These tools provide that support in a systematic, evidence-based way.

The "Triangle of Health"—gut, stress and sleep—forms your foundation. The nutritional protocols address widespread deficiencies. The biohacking tools optimize your biology. The tracking systems ensure you're moving in the right direction.

Most importantly, you don't have to do this alone. Whether you're working with a functional medicine practitioner, using online resources or building your own support network, the key is to stay consistent, stay curious and never give up on your body's amazing ability to heal itself.

Your Transformation Toolkit is complete, and now it's time to use it. These guidelines offer you a powerful resource—clear steps, proven strategies and practical insights to begin transforming your health. But we know that for many, pulling it all together can feel overwhelming. That's why we developed the Connected Health Program: a curated, personalized experience for those who want more than just information. With advanced lab testing and expert guidance, we create a tailored protocol based on your unique biology and goals. If you're ready to move from information to transformation, then check out Connected Health on our resource page to see if this is the right next step for you.

Progress, Not Perfection

You *will* have setbacks. That's part of the process. But instead of seeing them as failures, view them as data. What triggered the slip? How can you adjust? Every challenge is a chance to learn and refine your approach.

Most importantly, *celebrate your wins*, no matter how small. Did you swap soda for water or kombucha at lunch? Amazing. Did you go to bed 15 minutes earlier? That's progress. Every small step is progress on your journey to success.

This journey is *yours*. It's not about someone else's diet or someone else's lifestyle—it's about what works for *you* in a way that feels sustainable. Keep coming back to the basics, checking in with yourself and making those tiny, meaningful shifts.

Now, take action. Choose one small step today—a food swap, a bedtime tweak or a stress reliever. Write it down. Try it for a week. See how you feel. You *can* reimagine your health, one tiny habit at a time.

And if you ever feel like you need a guide along the way— someone to walk beside you, to help you make those small changes that lead to big results—I've got you covered. I've created a patient-centered program called Connected Health. This health collective is designed to support people just like you in making sustainable, personalized shifts that truly transform health over time. And part of designing this program has been centering on our patients' needs and filling in the gaps of care that they've encountered along the way.

Transformation happens through consistent daily actions, not perfection.

Here's how to implement these protocols systematically:

Week One

Foundation Setting

- Begin health journaling daily
- Start basic supplementation (vitamin D, magnesium, omega-3)
- Eliminate obvious inflammatory foods (processed foods, vegetable oils)
- Establish a consistent bedtime routine
- Gather and organize all existing health records
- Create your master health timeline
- Evaluate your current provider team for gaps and strengths
- Begin daily health tracking with standardized metrics

Week Two

Gut Health Focus

- Add fermented foods to daily meals
- Begin elimination diet if food sensitivities suspected
- Increase fiber through vegetables and low-sugar fruits
- Add digestive support supplements if needed

Team Optimization

- Research and interview potential new providers
- Schedule overdue preventive care appointments
- Review insurance benefits and coverage options
- Establish communication preferences with all providers

Week Three

Stress Management

- Implement daily breathwork practice (five to 10 minutes)
- Add gentle movement or stretching
- Begin stress-reduction techniques (meditation, journaling, nature walks)
- Evaluate and address major stressors

System Development

- Implement advanced documentation strategies
- Practice strategic communication techniques at upcoming appointments
- Create emergency preparedness plans
- Join relevant patient communities and advocacy groups

Week Four

Optimization

- Add advanced supplements based on individual needs
- Implement biohacking tools that appeal to you
- Fine-tune protocols based on journal observations
- Plan for long-term sustainability

Integration

- Conduct first quarterly review of progress
- Adjust systems based on early experience
- Plan next three months of health priorities

Beyond 30 Days: Long-Term Success

Monthly Assessments:

- Review progress and adjust protocols
- Add new interventions gradually
- Address barriers to consistency
- Celebrate victories and learn from setbacks

Quarterly Deep Dives:

- Consider comprehensive lab testing
- Evaluate supplement needs
- Assess goals and priorities
- Plan next level of optimization

The transformation from passive patient to strategic health advocate doesn't happen overnight, but the investment pays dividends for the rest of your life. You're not just improving your own care—you're modeling a new standard of patient engagement that elevates health-care for everyone.

One of my dreams, and a professional goal, is to meet everyone where they are. If you are a seasoned do-it-yourselfer, we have our website and free tools found in this book (**AaronHartmanMD.com**). If you need some help along the way or just don't have access to a functional medicine provider in your area, we have our online program Connected Health. If you just want to work with someone in person, you can come to my clinic. And if you want to take it to the next level and get the kind of time and attention that Anna has had over the last 18 years, we have our Personalized Precision Medicine program. I started on this ecosystem in 2016, so it has been a long time in the making.

Your health is too important to leave entirely in someone else's hands, no matter how qualified they may be. By developing these advocacy skills, you ensure that you'll always be your own best advocate, regardless of what health challenges you may face.

The system needs patients who think strategically, communicate effectively and refuse to accept substandard care. Be one of those patients. Your future self will thank you.

For access to our companion guide that will help walk you through all the above, please use the QR code below to access our book resources page.

24

AN INVITATION

I shared with you about how this past spring, Anna surprised all of us by swimming on her own for 30 minutes without a life preserver, then climbing out on her own—without help. Here's what hit me: At 19, Anna isn't just surviving—she's still improving. Still growing. Still defying every prediction ever made about her future. This wasn't a one-time fluke. She's been building toward this moment for years through daily physical therapy, electrical stimulation, targeted nutrition and sheer determination. But seeing her achieve this level of independence in the water—something that requires coordination, strength and confidence—reminded me that the human capacity for healing and growth never stops, even when experts say it should.

If that's possible for Anna, imagine what's possible for you.

The Real Choice: Pay the Farmer or Pay the Doctor

I learned something profound from a patient a few years ago that changed how I think about healthcare investments. She was facing a choice between spending $1200 on organic, grass-fed food for her family each month or keeping her current $800 grocery budget. She was worried about the extra cost.

Six months later, she sent me a note: "Dr. Hartman, my family hasn't been to the doctor once since we changed our food. My kids missed zero school days this year. My husband's energy is through the roof. I calculated it—we've saved over $3000 in medical bills and lost wages. That 'expensive' food was the best investment we ever made."

This is the choice every family faces: Pay the farmer now, or pay the doctor later.

Here's the reality check:

- Quality organic food costs about $300 to $850 more per month than processed food.
- The average family spends $4500 to $5500 annually on out of pocket medical expenses.
- One emergency room visit costs $2000 to $10000.
- Managing diabetes costs $13000+ per year per person.
- Treating heart disease costs $15000+ annually per person.

When you invest in real food, you're not just buying groceries—you're purchasing insurance against the diseases that bankrupt families and steal years from their lives.

After reading through these chapters, you might be feeling a bit overwhelmed. Functional medicine, biohacking, advocacy strategies, finding the right practitioners, navigating insurance—it's a lot. Even for someone who considers themselves health-savvy, the sheer volume of information can feel paralyzing.

You might be thinking:

"Where do I even start?"
"How do I know if I'm doing this right?"
"I don't have time to become a health expert."
"This seems complicated and expensive."

These are all valid concerns. The truth is, when I started this journey with Anna 19 years ago, I felt the same way. Even as a physician, I was overwhelmed by how much I didn't know about real healing.

That's exactly why we created **Connected Health**.

Connected Health: Your Simple Path Forward

After five years of development and working alongside thousands of patients, we've created what I wish had existed when Anna was first diagnosed. Connected Health isn't just another health program —it's your personal bridge from overwhelming information to clear, actionable steps that actually work.

Most health programs give you information and hope you figure out how to use it. But information without implementation is just entertainment. You need clarity on where to start, step-by-step guidance and support when things get confusing.

We start with your "Triangle of Health" assessment—the gut, stress and sleep framework that accounts for 80 percent of your healing potential. Within minutes, you'll know exactly which area needs attention first.

Your personalized roadmap gives you specific, actionable steps for the next 30 days. No guessing, no information overload—just clear direction based on your unique situation.

A curated community where tough questions get answered ensures you're making progress. When you hit sticking points or feel confused, you have access to clarification and support. Like having a functional medicine coach and experienced community in your pocket. Access the same resources my clinic patients use: guides, protocols, lab testing at reduced prices and direct access to our team when you need support.

Within your first week, you'll likely notice better sleep, improved energy and greater mental clarity. By day 30, most people experience significant improvement in their number one health concern and confidence in making health decisions.

This isn't about perfection—it's about progress. Real, measurable progress that builds on itself week after week.

What This Journey Really Gives You

Anna's transformation wasn't just about walking or talking or swimming. It was about possibility. About refusing to accept limitations as permanent. About discovering that labels like "uncurable" are often just descriptions of what hasn't been tried yet.

Your health journey is the same. Yes, you'll likely experience better energy, improved mood and enhanced vitality. But the real gift is something deeper: **the knowledge that you have more power over your biology and your future than you ever imagined.**

When you take charge of your health, you don't just change your body—you change your relationship with possibility itself. You stop accepting "That's just how it is" as an answer. You start believing in transformation, not just for your health, but for every area of your life.

You become someone who doesn't wait for permission to create the life they want. Someone who sees obstacles as puzzles to solve rather than walls that can't be climbed. Someone who models for their family and friends what's possible when you refuse to settle.

The Ripple Effect

Anna's story didn't just transform our family—it changed my entire approach to medicine and has influenced thousands of patients over the years. Your health transformation will have the same ripple effect.

Your children will grow up watching a parent who takes ownership of their health. Your spouse will see that vitality and energy are possible at any age. Your friends will witness what happens when someone refuses to accept "normal" aging and chronic disease as inevitable.

Every choice you make, every improvement you experience, every story you share becomes evidence for others that transformation is possible. You become living proof that "uncurable" doesn't mean "untreatable," that aging doesn't have to mean declining and that optimal health isn't reserved for the genetically gifted or financially privileged.

The Time Is Now

Here's what I know after 25 years of practice: The best time to start was 20 years ago. The second best time is right now.

My family's journey has been a wild ride of peaks and valleys. The benefits have been profound—I've helped my children avoid unnecessary procedures, found treatments that address root causes rather than just masking symptoms and taken complete control over my family's health narrative. Most significantly, it transformed my entire approach to practicing medicine.

But I won't sugarcoat the challenges. This path can be intensely isolating. We didn't have the support network I'm recommending to you in this book—it was just my wife and me navigating uncharted waters. Our social circle contracted as friends stopped inviting us to gatherings because our dietary requirements seemed strange or inconvenient. Kids' birthday parties, neighborhood barbecues, holiday meals—the invitations gradually disappeared.

Even more painful were the tensions that developed with family members who felt uncomfortable around us. They saw the remarkable progress in our children and compared it to their own kids' struggles, sometimes experiencing guilt or defensiveness rather than curiosity. These dynamics created distance with people we loved deeply.

This isolation period lasted about a decade, and it tested us emotionally, physically and spiritually. I share this not to discourage you, but to provide an honest picture—this journey isn't all unicorns and butterflies. There will be moments when you question everything.

Yet standing on the other side now, I can tell you with absolute certainty: Every challenge was worth it. Our struggle not only transformed our family's trajectory but has created ripple effects through everyone we've encountered—including you, reading these words right now. That makes even the hardest days meaningful. The treasure we found wasn't just better health—it was the ability to light the path for others. Remember, as Joseph Campbell and Bill Moyers say in *The Power of Myth,* "The cave you fear to enter holds the treasure you seek."

You don't need perfect conditions. You don't need unlimited resources. You don't need to wait until you have more time, more money or more motivation. You need to start where you are with what you have and build momentum through action.

Anna didn't wait for the perfect treatment or ideal circumstances. She worked with what we could provide and built on small improvements week after week, year after year. Today, at 19, she's still improving because she never stopped moving forward.

Your health is the foundation for everything else you want to accomplish in life. Your relationships, your career, your dreams, your ability to serve others—all of it depends on having the energy and vitality to show up fully for your life.

Every day you delay is a day of potential energy, joy and vitality that you don't get back. But every day you invest in your health creates a compound return that benefits you for the rest of your life.

You have a choice to make right now. You can close this book, feel inspired for a few days and then gradually return to the same patterns that brought you here. Or you can decide that today—this moment—is when your health transformation begins.

Anna's story proves that transformation is possible, even in the most challenging circumstances. Your story can prove the same thing. But only if you start.

Today, right now, make one choice that moves you toward better health. Start your health journal. Schedule that appointment. Eliminate that inflammatory food. Join Connected Health.

Do something. Your future self is counting on the decision you make at this moment.

Your health revolution doesn't begin with the perfect plan. It begins with a single choice to start.

What will you choose?

ACKNOWLEDGMENTS

This book is dedicated to my daughter, Anna. You have taught me more about the practice of medicine than any textbook, classroom or professor. Your hard work, amazing personality and infectious smile are still an inspiration to me today. You never give up and you do hard things; you are a true Hartman. I am still being taught by you, even today.

And to my wife Becky: You have nudged me, sometimes begrudgingly, down this path for more than 20 years. Whether it was fostering a disabled little girl who would later become our daughter, changing our diet at home and removing cleaning chemicals from our house, suggesting to me to put up a shingle for a functional medicine practice, saying I should go out on my own and start Central Virginia's first functional medicine practice, taking over my operations and designing an amazing practice and workspace or getting me involved with business masterminds to expand my vision for who we could help and how—we did this together. I couldn't have accomplished any of this without you.

And to my patients: You have allowed me to learn as I practice medicine, sometimes learning something days before I start to use it in my clinical practice, and at other times remembering key parts of your story while I'm reading—then sending a message through the portal in the wee hours. You have brought me research articles, been patient with the gaps in my knowledge base as I learn and stuck with me in your healing journey. After 24 years of this, I'm still practicing medicine.

Soli Deo Gloria

REFERENCES

Abir, Mahshid. 2025. "Combating America's Chronic Disease Epidemic." *RAND Corporation*. https://www.rand.org/pubs/commentary/2025/03/combating-americas-chronic-disease-epidemic.html.

Agostini, Lidiane P., Raquel S. Dettogni, Raquel S. dos Reis, Elaine Stur, Eldamária V. W. dos Santos, Diego P. Ventorim, Fernanda M. Garcia, Rodolfo C. Cardoso, Jones B. Graceli, and Iúri D. Louro. 2020. "Effects of Glyphosate Exposure on Human Health: Insights from Epidemiological and in Vitro Studies." *Science of the Total Environment* 705: 135808. https://doi.org/10.1016/j.scitotenv.2019.135808.

Allison, Lynn C. 2025. "Half of Americans Do Not Get Enough Magnesium." *Newsmax*. https://www.newsmax.com/health/health-news/magnesium-diet-soil/2025/04/03/id/1205502/.

American Psychological Association. 2023. "Stress in America™ 2023: A Nation Grappling with Psychological Impacts of Collective Trauma." *American Psychological Association*. https://www.apa.org/news/press/releases/2023/11/psychological-impacts-collective-trauma.

Barandouzi, Zahra A., Joochul Lee, Maria del Carmen Rosas, Jie Chen, Wendy A. Henderson, Angela R. Starkweather, and Xiaomei S. Cong. 2022. "Associations of neurotransmitters and the gut microbiome with emotional distress in mixed type of irritable bowel syndrome." *Scientific Reports*. 12, 1648. https://www.nature.com/articles/s41598-022-05756-0.

Barnett, Michael L., Zirui Song, and Bruce E. Landon. 2012. "Trends in Physician Referrals in the United States, 1999-2009." *Archives of Internal Medicine*. 172(2):163-170. https://doi.org/10.1001/archinternmed.2011.722.

Beidelschies, Michelle, Marilyn Alejandro-Rodriguez, Ning Guo, Anna Postan, Tawny Jones, Elizabeth Bradley, Mark Hyman, and Michael B. Rothberg. 2021. "Patient Outcomes and Costs Associated with Functional Medicine-Based Care in a Shared Versus Individual Setting for Patients with Chronic Conditions: A Retrospective Cohort Study." *BMJ Open*. 11: e048294. https://doi.org/10.1136/bmjopen-2020-048294.

Beidelschies, Michelle, Marilyn Alejandro-Rodriguez, Xinge Ji, Brittany Lapin, Patrick Hanaway, and Michael B. Rothberg. 2019. "Association of the Functional Medicine Model of Care with Patient-Reported Health-Related Quality-of-Life Outcomes." *JAMA Network Open*. 2(10): e1914017. https://doi.org/10.1001/jamanetworkopen.2019.14017.

Berwick, Donald M., Thomas W. Nolan, and John Whittington. 2008. "The Triple Aim: Care, Health, and Cost." *Health Affairs*. 27(3). https://www.healthaffairs.org/doi/10.1377/hlthaff.27.3.759.

Braut, Beatrice, and Marta Zatta. 2023. "Hand Hygiene: Semmelweis' Lesson Through

Céline's Pen." *Journal of Public Health*, 45(3): e574-e576. https://doi.org/10.1093/pubmed/fdado35.

Brooks, Jordan, Steven Day, Robert Shavelle, and David Strauss. 2011. "Low Weight, Mortality, and Mortality in Children With Cerebral Palsy: New Clinical Growth Charts." *Pediatrics: Official Journal of the American Academy of Pediatrics*. https://doi.org/ 10.1542/peds.2010-2801, and https://www.lifeexpectancy.org/articles/Growth Charts2. pdf.

Burhans, MS. 2018. "Vitamin B12 Status: Are Genetics a Driving Factor?" Fred Hutch Cancer Center. https://www.fredhutch.org/en/news/spotlight/2018/06/phs_hu_blood.html.

Camilleri, Michael. 2019. "Leaky Gut: Mechanisms, Measurement and Clinical Implications in Humans." *Gut*. 68(8): 1519-1526. https://doi.org/10.1136/gutjnl-2019-318427.

Cappuccio, Francesco P., Lanfranco D'Elia, Pasquale Strazzullo, and Michelle A. Miller. 2010. "Sleep Duration and All-Cause Mortality: A Systematic Review and Meta-Analysis of Prospective Studies." *Sleep*, 33(5): 585-592. https://doi.org/10.1093/sleep/33.5.585.

Cassella, Carly. 2024. "The Mysterious Case of the Youngest Person Ever Diagnosed With Alzheimer's." *ScienceAlert*. https://www.sciencealert.com/the-mysterious-case-of-the-youngest-person-ever-diagnosed-with-alzheimers.

Cazorla-González, Jorge, Sergi García-Retortillo, Mariano Gacto-Sánchez, Gerard Muñoz-Castro, Juan Serrano-Ferrer, Blanca Román-Viñas, Abel López-Bermejo, Raquel Font-Lladó, and Anna Prats-Puig. 2022. "Effects of Crawling Before Walking: Network Interactions and Longitudinal Associations in 7-Year-Old Children." *International Journal of Environmental Research and Public Health*, 19(9): 5561. https://doi.org/10.3390/ijerph19095561.

Center for Disease Control (CDC). 2024. "FastStats: Sleep in Adults." CDC.gov. https://www.cdc.gov/sleep/data-research/facts-stats/adults-sleep-facts-and-stats.html.

Center for Disease Control (CDC). 2025. "Data and Statistics on Autism Spectrum Disorder." CDC.gov. https://www.cdc.gov/autism/data-research/index.html.

Center for Disease Control (CDC). 2025. "Leading Causes of Death (for US)." CDC.gov. https://www.cdc.gov/nchs/fastats/leading-causes-of-death.htm.

Chen, Junshi. 2012. "An Original Discovery: Selenium Deficiency and Keshan Disease (An Endemic Heart Disease)." *Asia Pacific Journal of Clinical Nutrition*, 21(3): 320-6. https://pubmed.ncbi.nlm.nih.gov/22705420/.

Cohen, Robin A. and Laryssa Mykyta, reporters. 2023. "Percentage of Adults Aged 18 Years and Older Who Took Prescription Medication During the Past 12 Months, by Sex and Age Group - National Health Interview Survey, United States, 2021." *Morbidity and Mortality Weekly Report*, 72(16): 450. https://doi.org/10.15585/mmwr.mm7216a7.

Crenner, Christopher. 2024. "Ulcers, Stress, and the Discovery of *Helicobacter pylori*." *The Lancet*, 403 (10444): 2586-2587. https://doi.org/10.1016/S0140-6736(24)01206-6.

Dickson, Stephen. n.d. "Low-Dose Naltrexone (LDN) and Traumatic Brain Injury." *LDN Research Trust*. https://ldnresearchtrust.org/low-dose-naltrexone-ldnpercent-C2percentAoand-traumatic-brain-injury.

Didier, Kevin, Loïs Bolko, Delphine Giusti, Segolene Toquet, Ailsa Robbins, Frank Antonicelli, and Amelie Servettaz. 2018. "Autoantibodies Associated With Connective Tissue Diseases: What Meaning for Clinicians?" *Frontiers In Immunology*, 9: 541. https://doi.org/10.3389/fimmu.2018.00541.

"Digestive Diseases Statistics for the United States." 2014. *National Institute of Diabetes and Digestive and Kidney Diseases.* https://www.niddk.nih.gov/health-information/health-statistics/digestive-diseases.

Dinan, Timothy, and John F. Cryan. 2016. "Gut Instincts: Microbiota as a Key Regulator of Brain Development, Ageing and Neurodegeneration. *The Journal of Physiology*, 595(2): 489-503. https://doi.org/10.1113/JP273106.

Drake, Victoria. 2018. "Micronutrient Inadequacies in the US Population: an Overview." Linus Pauling Institute, Oregon State University. https://lpi.oregonstate.edu/mic/micronutrient-inadequacies/overview.

"EMFs: Health Impacts and Reducing Exposures." 2024. *The Institute for Functional Medicine.* https://www.ifm.org/articles/emf-health-reducing-exposures.

"Evidence Based Medicine." 2025. Stony Brook University Libraries. https://guides.library.stonybrook.edu/medicine/ebm.

"FDA to Revoke Authorization for the Use of Red No. 3 in Food and Ingested Drugs." 2025. U. S. Food & Drug Administration. https://www.fda.gov/food/hfp-constituent-updates/fda-revoke-authorization-use-red-no-3-food-and-ingested-drugs.

Fogg, B.J. 2020. *Tiny Habits: The Small Changes That Change Everything.* Houghton Mifflin Harcourt.

Fugh-Berman, Adriane. 2021. "Industry-Funded Medical Education is Always Promoted." *BMJ*, 373(1273). https://doi.org/10.1136/bmj.n1273.

Green, Rivka, Bruce Lanphear, and Richard Hornung. 2019. "Association Between Maternal Fluoride Exposure During Pregnancy and IQ Scores in Offspring in Canada." *JAMA Pediatrics*, 173(10): 940-948. https://doi.org/10.1001/jamapediatrics.2019.1729.

Greger, Michael. 2013. "98 percent of American Diets Potassium-Deficient." *NutritionFacts.org.* https://nutritionfacts.org/blog/98-of-american-diets-potassium-deficient/.

Gussak, Ihor B., John B. Kostis, Ibrahim Akin, and Martin Borggrefe, eds. 2017. *Iatrogenicity: Causes and Consequences of Iatrogenesis in Cardiovascular Medicine.* Rutgers University Press Medicine.

Igbinigie, Precious O., Ruoling Chen, Jie Tang, Alexandru Dregan, Jiaqian Yin, Dev Acharya, Rizwan Nadim, Anthony Chen, Zhongliang Bai, and Farzad Amirabdollahian. 2024. "Association Between Egg Consumption and Dementia in Chinese Adults." *Nutrients*, 16(19): 3340. https://doi.org/10.3390/nu16193340.

Ioannidis, John P. A. 2025. "Why Most Published Research Findings Are False." *PLOS Medicine*, 19(8): e1004085. https://doi.org/10.1371/journal.pmed.1004085.

Jarry, Jonathan. 2024. "You Probably Don't Have Leaky Gut." *McGill Office for Science and Society.* https://www.mcgill.ca/oss/article/medical-critical-thinking/you-probably-dont-have-leaky-gut.

Kresser, Chris. 2018. "Well Fed but Undernourished: An American Epidemic." Kresser

Institute. https://kresserinstitute.com/well-fed-but-undernourished-an-american-epidemic/.

Lam, Matt. 2025. "Poor Sleep Alters Immune Cells, Increasing Risk for Inflammatory Diseases." *Neuroscience News.* https://neurosciencenews.com/slep-deprivation-immune-system-28436/.

Lauderdale, Diane S. 2015. "Are Americans Sleeping Less Than They Used To? Evidence for Adults and Adolescents." University of Chicago Biological Sciences. https://conference.nber.org/confer/2016/CSs16/Lauderdale.pdf.

Macura, Barbara, Aneta Kiecka, and Marian Szczepanik. 2024. "Intestinal Permeability Disturbances: Causes, Diseases and Therapy." *Clinical and Experimental Medicine,* 24(232). https://doi.org/10.1007/s10238-024-01496-9.

Makary, Martin, and Michael Daniel. 2016. "Medical Error: The Third Leading Cause of Death in the US." *BMJ,* 353: i2139. https://doi.org/10.1136/bmj.i2139.

Makary, Marty. 2024. *Blind Spots: When Medicine Gets It Wrong, and What It Means for Our Health.* Bloomsbury Publishing.

Martin, Crescent B., Craig M. Hales, Qiuping Gu, and Cynthia L. Ogden. 2019. "Prescription Drug Use in the United States, 2015-2016." *NCHS Data Brief,* 334. https://www.cdc.gov/nchs/products/databriefs/db334.htm.

McEwen, Bruce S. 2007. "Physiology and Neurobiology of Stress and Adaptation: Central Role of the Brain." *Physiological Reviews,* 87(3): 873-904. https://doi.org/10.1152/physrev.00041.2006.

McGough, Matt, Imani Telesford, Aubrey Winger, Lynne Cotter, and Cynthia Cox. 2024. "How Much is Health Spending Expected to Grow?" *Health System Tracker.* https://www.healthsystemtracker.org/chart-collection/how-much-is-health-spending-expected-to-grow/.

Medithi, Srujana, Yogeswar Dayal Kasa, Vijay Radhakrishna Kankipati, Venkiah Kodali, Babban Jee, and Padmaja R. Jonnalagadda. 2022. "Impact of Micronutrient Supplementation on Pesticide Residual, Acetylcholinesterase Activity, and Oxidative Stress Among Farm Children Exposed to Pesticides." *Frontiers in Public Health,* 10:872125. https://doi.org/10.3389/fpubh.2022.872125.

Meerlo, Peter, Andrea Sgoifo, and Deborah Suchecki. 2008. "Restricted and Disrupted Sleep: Effects on Autonomic Function, Neuroendocrine Stress Systems and Stress Responsivity." *Sleep Medicine Reviews,* 12(3): 197-210. https://doi.org/10.1016/j.smrv.2007.07.007.

Monteiro, C.A, J. C. Moubarac, G. Cannon, S. W. Ng, and B. Popkin. 2013. "Ultra-Processed Products are Becoming Dominant in the Global Food System." *Obesity Reviews,* 14(S2): 21-28. https://doi.org/10.1111/obr.12107.

Mowat, Allan, and William W. Agace. 2014. "Regional Specialization Within the Intestinal Immune System." *Nature Reviews Immunology,* 14: 667-685. https://doi.org/10.1038/nri3738.

"National Health Expenditure Projections 2015-2025." *Centers for Medicare and Medicaid.* https://www.cms.gov/research-statistics-data-and-systems/statistics-trends-and-reports/nationalhealthexpenddata/downloads/proj2015.pdf.

"National Research Council (2006)." Fluoride Action Network. https://fluoridealert.org/researchers/nrc/findings/.

Nijssen, Kevin M. R., Ronald P. Mensink, Jogchum Plat, and Peter J. Joris. 2023. "Longer-Term Mixed Nut Consumption Improves Brain Vascular Function and Memory (A Randomized, Controlled Crossover Trial in Older Adults)." *Clinical Nutrition*, 42(7): 1067-1075. https://doi.org/10.1016/j.clnu.2023.05.025.

Oghbaei, Morteza, Jamuna Prakash, and Fatih Yildiz. 2016. "Effect of Primary Processing of Cereals and Legumes on its Nutritional Quality: A Comprehensive Review." *Cogent Food & Agriculture*, 2(1). https://doi.org/10.1080/23311932.2015.1136015.

Pan, Yongyi, Taylor C. Wallace, Tasija Karosas, David A. Bennett, Puja Agarwal, and Mei Chung. 2024. "Association of Egg Intake With Alzheimer's Dementia Risk in Older Adults: The Rush Memory and Aging Project." *Journal of Nutrition* 154(7): 2236-2243. https://doi.org/10.1016/j.tjnut.2024.05.012.

Papanikolaou, Yanni, James Brooks, Carroll Reider, and Victor L. Fulgoni III. 2014. "U.S. Adults are Not Meeting Recommended Levels for Fish and Omega-3 Fatty Acid Intake: Results of an Analysis Using Observational Data from NHANES 2003–2008." *Nutrition Journal* 13(31). https://doi.org/10.1186/1475-2891-13-31.

"Pediatric Feeding and Swallowing Program." 2025. University of Alabama. https://shc.cd.ua.edu/programs/pediatric-feeding-program/.

Pickering, Gisèle, André Mazur, Marion Trousselard, Przemyslaw Bienkowski, Natalia Yaltsewa, Mohamed Amessou, Lionel Noah, and Etienne Pouteau. 2020. "Magnesium Status and Stress: The Vicious Circle Concept Revisited." *Nutrients*, 12(12): 3672. https://doi.org/10.3390/nu12123672.

Qato, Dima, Katharine Ozenberger, and Mark Olfson. 2018. "Prevalence of Prescription Medications With Depression as a Potential Adverse Effect Among Adults in the United States." *JAMA* 319(22): 2289-2298. https://doi.org/10.1001/jama.2018.6741.

Rothberg, Michael B., Joshua Class, Tara F. Bishop, Jennifer Friderici, Reva Kleppel, and Peter K. Lindenauer. 2014. "The Cost of Defensive Medicine on Three Hospital Medicine Services." *JAMA Internal Medicine*, 174(11): 1867-8. https://doi.org/10.1001/jamainternmed.2014.4649.

Ruel, Guillaume, Sonia Pomerleau, Patrick Couture, Simone Lemieux, Benoît Lamarche, and Charles Couillard. 2008. "Low-Calorie Cranberry Juice Supplementation Reduces Plasma Oxidized LDL and Cell Adhesion Molecule Concentrations in Men." *British Journal of Nutrition*, 99(2): 352-359. https://doi.org/10.1017/S0007114507811986.

Rupp, Adam, Erin Young, and Andrea L. Chadwick. 2023. "Low-Dose Naltrexone's Utility for Non-Cancer Centralized Pain Conditions: A Scoping Review." *Pain Medicine*, 24(11): 1270-1287. https://doi.org/10.1093/pm/pnad074.

Sackett, David L., William M. C. Rosenberg, J. A. Muir Gray, R. Brian Haynes, and W. Scott Richardson. 1996. "Evidence Based Medicine: What It Is and What It Isn't." *BMJ*, 312:71. https://doi.org/10.1136/bmj.312.7023.71.

Scheer, Roddy, and Doug Moss. 2011. "Dirt Poor: Have Fruits and Vegetables Become Less Nutritious?" *Scientific American*. https://www.scientificamerican.com/article/soil-depletion-and-nutrition-loss/.

Shaw, Rachel L., Gemma Heath, Virginia Eatough, and Lisa Thackeray. 2025. "Parental Intuition: A Phenomenological Structure of Intuitive Knowing in the Context of Child Illness and Shared Decision-Making in Healthcare." *International Journal of Qualitative Studies on Health and Well-Being*, 20(1): 2491925. https://doi.org/10.1080/17482631.2025.2491925.

Shoenfeld, Yehuda, Nancy Agmon-Levin, and Lucija Tomljenovic, eds. 2015. *Vaccines and Autoimmunity*. Wiley.

Slavich, George M., and Steven W. Cole. 2013. "The Emerging Field of Human Social Genomics." *Clinical Psychological Science* 1(3): 331-348. https://doi.org/10.1177/2167702613478594.

"Sleep Health." n.d. National Heart, Lung and Blood Institute, National Institutes of Health. https://www.nhlbi.nih.gov/health-topics/education-and-awareness/sleep-health.

Sullivan, Dan, and Benjamin Hardy. 2021. *The Gap and the Gain: The High Achievers' Guide to Happiness, Confidence, and Success*. Hay House.

Tan, Hui-Leng, Leila Kheirandish-Gozal, and David Gozal. 2019. "Sleep, Sleep Disorders and Immune Function." *Allergy and Sleep*, edited by Anna Fishbein and Stephen H. Sheldon. https://doi.org/10.1007/978-3-030-14738-9_1.

Tang, Ying, Minji Xu, and Shiu-Ming Kuo. 2018. "Factors Contributing to the High Prevalence of Vitamin B6 Deficiency in the US." *Journal of Human Nutrition*, 2(1): 58-64. https://doi.org/10.36959/487/282.

Taylor, Kyla W., Sorina E. Eftim, and Christopher A. Sibrizzi. 2025. "Fluoride Exposure and Children's IQ Scores: A Systematic Review and Meta-Analysis." *JAMA Pediatrics*, 179(3): 282-292. https://doi.org/10.1001/jamapediatrics.2024.5542.

Teitelbaum, Jacob. 2021. "Eliminating Candida Overgrowth." *Newsmax*. https://www.newsmax.com/Health/jacobteitelbaum/candida-fatigue-fibromyalgia-infection/2021/03/26/id/1015354/.

Tin, Alexander. 2024. "Federal Court Rules Against EPA in Lawsuit Over Fluoride in Water." CBS News. https://www.cbsnews.com/news/epa-fluoride-drinking-water-federal-court-ruling/.

Toljan, Karlo, and Bruce Vrooman. 2018. "Low-Dose Naltrexone (LDN): Review of Therapeutic Utilization." *Medical Sciences*, 6(4): 82. https://doi.org/10.3390/medsci6040082.

Van Den Bos, Jill, Karan Rustagi, Travis Gray, Michael Halford, Eva Ziemkiewicz, and Jonathan Shreve. 2011. "The $17.1 Billion Problem: The Annual Cost Of Measurable Medical Errors." *Health Affairs*, 30(4). https://doi.org/10.1377/hlthaff.2011.0084.

van der Kolk, Bessel A. 2014. *The Body Keeps the Score*. Viking.

Watson, Kathleen B., Jennifer L. Wiltz, Kunthea Nhim, Rachel B. Kaufmann, Craig W. Thomas, and Kurt J. Greenlund. 2025. "Trends in Multiple Chronic Conditions Among US Adults, By Life Stage, Behavioral Risk Factor Surveillance System, 2013–2023." *Preventing Chronic Disease*, 22(E15). https://doi.org/10.5888/pcd22.240539.

Weich, Scott, Peter Croft, Ilana Crome, and Martin Fridher. 2014. "Effect of Anxiolytic and Hypnotic Drug Prescriptions on Mortality Hazards: Retrospective Cohort Study." *BMJ* 348: g1996. https://www.bmj.com/content/348/bmj.g1996.

Wu, Chuyue, Yixun Ke, and Roch A. Nianogo. 2025. "Trends in Hyperinsulinemia and Insulin Resistance Among Nondiabetic US Adults, NHANES, 1999–2018." *Journal of Clinical Medicine*, 14(9): 3215. https://doi.org/10.3390/jcm14093215.

Younger, Jarred, Luke Parkityny, and David McLain. 2014. "The Use of Low-Dose Naltrexone as a Novel Anti-Inflammatory Treatment for Chronic Pain." *Clinical Rheumatology*, 33: 451-459. https://doi.org/10.1007/s10067-014-2517-2.

Zhang, Han, Jiangyu Wang, Shuting Tian, Wenhui Hao, and Lingjuan Du. 2022. "Two B-Box Proteins, MaBBX20 and MaBBX51, Coordinate Light-Induced Anthocyanin Biosynthesis in Grape Hyacinth." *International Journal of Molecular Sciences*, 23(10): 5678. https://doi.org/10.3390/ijms23105678.

Zhang, Jenny. 2024. "Why Don't Americans Eat Organ Meats? Exploring the Surprising Absence of Offal in the American Diet." *ScientificOrigin*. https://scientificorigin.com/why-dont-americans-eat-organ-meat-exploring-the-surprising-absence-of-offal-in-the-american-diet.

ABOUT THE AUTHOR

Dr. Aaron Hartman was a father desperately searching for answers whose experience with his daughter transformed him from a traditional military physician into a revolutionary functional medicine doctor. Now triple board-certified in Family Medicine, Integrative Medicine and Anti-Aging/Regenerative/Metabolic Medicine, Dr. Hartman has helped thousands recover from "uncurable" conditions, including autoimmune diseases, chronic Lyme, POTS and mold illness.

His Richmond, Virginia functional medicine practice pioneered treating root causes when conventional medicine said nothing more could be done. By combining cutting-edge science with forgotten nutritional wisdom, he's created reproducible protocols that turn medical impossibilities into everyday miracles.

For more information about Dr. Aaron Hartman and *UnCurable*, scan the QR code below

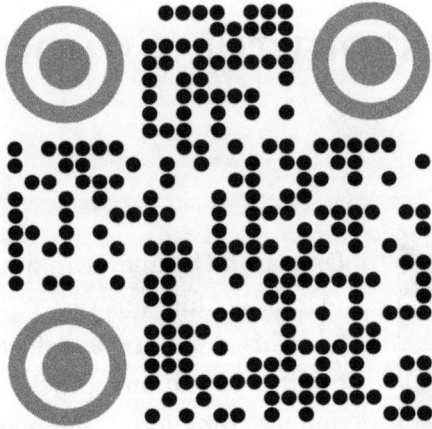

ABOUT THE PUBLISHER

Legacy Launch Pad is a boutique publishing company that works with entrepreneurs from all over the world.

For more information about Legacy Launch Pad Publishing, go to: www.legacylaunchpadpub.com.